THE MAN WHO KNEW

THE MAN WHO KNEW

By

RALPH WALDO TRINE

Printed in the United States of America and Australia.

Bottom of the Hill Publishing
Memphis, TN
www.BottomoftheHillPublishing.com

ISBN: 978-1-61203-401-0

CONTENTS

Chapter 1
The Time, The Place, The Need, the Man

There are supreme and epoch-making moments in the life of the world. There are supreme and light and power-bringing moments in the lives of individuals.

A supreme moment in the life of the world is when some great prophet, seer, sage, or saviour appears with a great elemental truth, and is able to impart it to others with a persuasive beauty and power.

A supreme moment in the lives of individuals is when they come face to face with such a truth — when it comes clearly and convincingly to them. Such truth must not only be uttered, but, to have authority and power, it must be lived by him who utters it. Moreover it must be a truth that becomes an inspiration and a real help in the daily lives of common men and women — men and women who have their problems to meet, their fears to face, their battles to fight, their bread to win.

The greatest saying in the world's history, when adequately understood, was given utterance by a young Palestinian Jew, some nineteen hundred years ago — and how short a time, comparatively, that is in the life of the human race.

He started life humbly, the son of a carpenter, and worked some years at his father's trade, but his life and influence became so great that time stopped and began again from the date of his birth; or rather, the measuring of time began again for practically the entire human race.

It is a life, if men were sensible, most easily understood; but by virtue of inherited mental and spiritual inhibitions it has become one of the most misunderstood in the world, and with an incalculable loss to the world.

A sympathetic and unbiased study of such a life would seem to be something of both interest and value — of real concrete value. Real greatness, lasting greatness, comes only through unusual human service. There must therefore be something unusually helpful in his life.

Reference has been made to 'the greatest saying in the world's history.' It fortunately took the form of a direct answer to a direct question that was put to him in public, so that many heard both question and answer. What were the facts surrounding this occurrence? For a full understanding of the statement, the following brief facts are essential:

The people of Judea were a portion of a race that had been devout and, as they felt, particularly favoured by Divine Providence. Many great prophets and teachers had appeared among them. They led primarily a pastoral life, which was conducive to the highest inspiration, and the inception, therefore, of a pure and vital type of religion. A strikingly large number of their prophets were husbandmen and shepherds.

Out in the open, tilling their fields, or herding their flocks, with their hearts and their minds open to the voice of their God, they made it possible for the revelation of great truths to come to them; and such revelations did come to them. We can recall numbers of wonderful sayings of Hebrew prophets, containing various elemental truths of life, many of them taking great beauty of form.

As time passed, however, their religion became stereotyped, as is so often and so generally the case. Organization, form, ceremony — and at times even cant and hypocrisy, with its established order of priests, scribes, and interpreters — took the place of the vital truths that had come from their prophets, open-windowed to their God. For close on three hundred years, through this deadening influence, no prophet had spoken.

All inspiration, and all chance for inspiration, had gone. The people became settled in the dead level of the commonplace, through tradition and dogma, nourished and systematically cultivated by a thoroughly entrenched ecclesiastical institution.

The priests, arrayed in their fine raiment, sat in the seats of authority and regarded themselves as something apart from the life of the people, and with a vested authority that made them not 'servants,' but would-be masters of the people.

All religious teaching emanating from them took set forms: 'It is said,' 'It is written,' 'Moses has said,' 'The prophets have said,' and even, 'Thus saith the Lord.' The soul's windows were not kept open to Jehovah as formerly. They were open, when open at all, toward Jerusalem, where ritual in its ever-increasing forms waxed stronger.

So the religious life of the people, and with it their entire life, became one where the spirit was dead. The empty form alone remained.

The priests and ecclesiastical orders became their overlords; and the condition of the people, as is always true in any country or nation where this comes about, was pitiable.

To add to their burdens, they had fallen under the yoke of an alien power — Rome. Tiberius Caesar was the Roman emperor. Under him was Pontius Pilate, the Roman governor or representative of Judea.

Rome conducted its campaigns — its raids threw great numbers of its captives into slavery, and exacted tribute, under its well-established policy of conquest. But Rome was already in its decadence, and its people required continually greater amounts to satisfy this desire for show, and all that wasteful expenditure summed up in the phrase panem et circenses.

This oppression, combined with the oppression of the ecclesiastical hierarchy, made the life and the condition of the people of Judea hard, discouraging, and pitiable. There was a tradition among them, which had persisted for some time, that a Deliverer would be sent them, and this, on account of their hard conditions, they were ready and even eager to believe.

Into these surroundings or conditions came a young Rabbi, or teacher, a successor once more to their long line of prophets; but one with such a supreme aptitude for discerning the things of the mind and the spirit that he became the greatest prophet, and therefore teacher, of them all.

He was the son, the eldest son, of poor but highly thought-of parents — Joseph and Mary. Joseph was a carpenter, in the little, and at that time comparatively unknown, village of Nazareth. There were four other sons, we are told, whose names were common names in the little village. There were daughters; how many and their names we are not told, but two are mentioned.

The eldest son was named Joshua (Jesus) and was known as Joshua Ben Joseph — Joshua son of Joseph. After the custom of the time and place, he followed the vocation of a carpenter, and as a carpenter worked with his father. What his schooling and his training were we do not know. Of this portion of his life, so important and so interesting, there is no record.

That his birth, the manner of his birth, and the manner of his life were at all different from those in the little community in which he lived and worked, was entirely unknown by those among whom he lived and worked, and later taught. 'Is not this the carpenter, the son of Mary, the brother of James, and Joses, and of Judas, and Simon? and are not his sisters here with us?' (Mark 6:3)

That he had a strong, vigorous, pleasing, and even compelling personality; that he had great vigour and independence of thought; that he loved and lived the life of the open; that he had a marked aptitude for discerning, and imparting in a compelling manner, the things of the spirit, we must believe, because the people — the common people — 'heard him gladly.' Some said that never man spoke as this man; and soon great multitudes began to follow him.

He had not only the power of interesting, leading, and teaching them, but also the power of healing, so that many who came to him he healed of their afflictions and diseases. He did this by arousing in them, as he very often stated, a certain power of 'faith,' which is a power of thought, so that the latent powers within them were so aroused and so directed that they were made whole — many even instantly.

At approximately thirty years of age, he appeared one day at a place where a cousin, named John — later called John the Baptist — who had spent a considerable time alone in the wilderness in preparation for the mission to which he felt called, was delivering a message to the people who had come out to hear him. He was of a vigorous personality and his message was: 'Prepare ye the way of the Lord, make his paths straight.' And again: 'Repent ye: for the Kingdom of Heaven is at hand.'

Through a rite of baptism — a custom very common in that country and at that time — he was inducting those who would into the new life that he set forth and that he called upon them to follow.

Jesus, among others, accepted baptism at the hands of John, and began almost immediately in a ministry of his own. The striking thing about him and his method, which attracted the attention of all and even astonished all, was that he cited no 'authority' for the truth that he put forth; but spoke as one having authority.

It was not 'It is written,' 'It has been said,' 'The prophets have said,' but 'I say unto you.' He gave what he himself perceived as truth, and the result was that it was with such persuasion and power, that all felt the authority with which he spoke. He claimed no 'supernatural' power for himself. He never made mention of it, and he chided those who would thrust it upon him.

What was his message that came with such authority and such moving power?

It was the message of discovery. A new era had come in the evolution, in the upward climb, the progress of the race. Or rather, perhaps, a new knowledge which, if followed, would of itself make for a new era. And this is the message that he gave, that he reiterated in the same form or in kindred forms, straight through to the end: 'The Kingdom of God is at hand: repent ye, and believe the Gospel.' Repent means to turn, Gospel means good news.

The Kingdom of God has come nigh. Sometimes he used the expression, the Kingdom of God, sometimes the expression, the Kingdom of Heaven, and by each he meant the same.

Repeatedly as he taught he gave the injunction: 'Seek ye first the Kingdom of God, and His righteousness; and all these things shall be added unto you.' And this was followed by a kindred injunction: 'Neither shall they say, Lo here! or Lo there! for, behold, the Kingdom of God is within you.' His conception and his express teaching of God is: 'God is Spirit.'

The Kingdom of God has came nigh - which I reveal to you. It is an inner kingdom — the conscious union of the human with the Divine. It is the revelation that the One life, the Divine life, the God life, which is Spirit, is the life that is within us.

To realize this Life as our life, to love it, and to live always in its realization, to open ourselves to its illumination, its guidance and its power, is the finding of the Kingdom of God, of the Kingdom of Heaven — the kingdom of harmony — that he perceived, lived, and revealed to the world.

It is the conscious vital realization of the essential oneness of each life with the universal Divine Life, that is the source and the essence of all life. It is to realize and always to live consciously in the state: 'In Him we live, and move, and have our being.'

The Divine essence, the Divine Centre of life came to him as 'Father.' His own realization was: The Father in me and I in the Father. His teaching was: 'As I am ye shall be.' Again his realization was: It is the Father that worketh in me, my Father works and I work. Then again, his teaching was as he so distinctly said: 'As I am ye shall be.'

His teaching took these lines: I show you the way, and it is idle for you to call me Lord and Master, unless you do the things I tell you. It is idle to say merely that you believe on me. That alone means nothing. But if you believe me, actually believe me, you will do the things I tell you to do; you will follow my commandments.

His injunction is, then, to become open-minded, open-hearted, open-windowed, to the God life, which is the life, the real life within — that it do for us what it does for him.

Again he said: 'Of myself I can do nothing. It is the Father that worketh in me; my Father works and I work.' And then again he enjoins that we live and work in the realization of the same relations with the Divine life within — the Father — and that if we do, we then realize his statement: 'Not only shall ye do these things; but greater things than these shall ye do'.

He, then, of all men, had a clear vision — and this made him the Great Teacher — of the reality of the human soul, of the indwelling of the Divine in the human, in the degree that the human realizes its true Self, and through desire and through will, which indicate his love for it, lives habitually in this realization and life.

It is the Fatherhood of God, and if the Fatherhood, then the Divine Sonship of man; and as a concomitant of this, there flows from it, and inevitably, the Brotherhood of Man.

That we realize the God life within us, the Kingdom of God within, that we love it, that we live in it, was his repeated command.

The life that he taught was questioned by some of his hearers; and one day, we are told, as he taught the people, a certain lawyer arose and asked a question. A 'lawyer' was a scribe, or an interpreter, and teacher of the ecclesiastical law and observances. His question was: 'Master, which is the great commandment in the law?' Jesus said unto him, 'Thou shalt love the Lord thy God with all thy heart, and with all thy soul, and with all thy mind. This is the first and great commandment. And the second is like unto it, Thou shalt love thy neighbour as thyself. On these two commandments hang all the law and the prophets.'

This to me, because fraught with such potency and power, is, when rightly understood, when interpreted in the light of his 'gospel,' his good news of the life, the Kingdom of God within, the greatest saying in the world's history.

It is significant to remember here also the words of the Master: 'Think not that I am come to destroy the law, or the prophets: I am not come to destroy, but to fulfill.'

As we read his words, 'Thou shalt love the Lord thy God,' we get far afield, unless we keep clearly in mind his teaching, that God is Spirit, which is Life, and that the Kingdom of God is within. His own perception of this truth was so clear, that he never conceived of his life as any other than the life of God, the Father.

He never recognized the fact that he had any life outside the Divine life within him — my Father — in Heaven. 'Believe me that I am in the Father, and the Father in me.' And again:

'The words I speak unto you I speak not of myself: but the Father abiding in me doeth His work.' And to those before him he said: 'Call no man your father upon the earth: for one is your Father, which is in Heaven.'

He never speaks of his life as any other than one with God, the

Father; and his constant injunction, even pleading injunction, is that all men so realize their lives. To him only in this conscious union with God was there reality.

The Kingdom of God and His righteousness is not only what he intended to teach, the basis of all of his revelation, but what he undoubtedly did teach — and that he so longed to establish in the minds and hearts of men. In more than thirty places he explains to his disciples, and to others, his mission and his purpose: to preach the glad tidings of the Kingdom of God.

Repeatedly the accounts of him read: 'He went about through cities and villages, preaching and bringing good tidings of the Kingdom of God.' And then later on: 'He sent them forth to Preach the Kingdom of God, and to heal the sick.' 'And this Gospel of the Kingdom shall be preached in the whole world for a testimony to all nations.'

His Divine self-realization was the reason, the secret, as he said, of his insight and his power. He taught always that the same results would be realized in the lives of all who lived in this same realization, this law, this way of life.

His own words are: 'He that believeth on me,' and shows it by living the same life, 'the works that I do shall he do also.' It was a clear-cut law of being, that he realized, lived, and then revealed to the world.

His finding, and his message to the world, was then that there is an order of life, 'The Way,' as he called it, whereby through the channel of our minds we can bring our thought, and therefore our lives as individual lives, into such harmony and union with the Universal Life that as it guides and cares for the planets in their courses, the sparrow in its flight, so it guides and cares for us. Live this life, said he, and then do not worry about your life.

When he said, 'My Father gives me all power because I seek to do the will of my Father,' he must have meant, 'because I seek constantly to live in mind and spirit in such harmony with my Father's life that I become an open channel through which His life and power can manifest themselves and work.' This perfect blending of the human with the Divine is his realization that makes him Master, Way-shower; and the knowledge of this is his gift to us. This is his truth, of which he says: 'Ye shall know the truth, and the truth shall make you free.'

Chapter 2
Getting This, You Have All

We are learning much of late of the finer forces of the universe and of life. The law underlying the finer forces that has made the radio possible, or rather our apprehension of that law, indicates still finer forces that we are yet to apprehend, understand, and formulate in terms of law.

Can we state the Master's fundamental teaching in the terms of law? Through our continually enlarging knowledge of the finer forces of the universe, within us and about us, the law can be stated in this form: The realization of the real Self — as the indwelling spirit of Life — brings about the condition wherein the individual life becomes a focal-point, and in turn a center of the Universal Life force. Becoming thus attuned to it, it takes to itself, in an ever- increasing degree, its qualities and its powers, and becomes thereby an ever-increasing centre of creative force and power.

It was that eminent English Churchman, Archdeacon Wilberforce, who said: 'The secret of optimism is the mental effort to abide in conscious oneness with the Supreme Power, the Infinite Immanent Mind evolving a perfect purpose . . . .Our slow-moving minds may be long in recognizing it, and our unspiritual lives may seem to contradict it; but deep in the center of the being of every man there is a divine self to be awakened, a ray of God's life which Paul calls "the Christ in you." Jesus is the embodiment of the universal principle of the immanence of God in man. Thus is Jesus the "Mediator," or uniting medium between God and man.

'The principle of what is called Christianity is the immanence of our Father-God in humanity; the fact that individual men are separate items in a vast solidarity in which Infinite Mind is expressing Himself. Jesus has shown us what the ideal is to which that principle will lead . . . . The mystic Christ will win us here or hereafter. To find him within us now, to let him conquer us now, to recognize him as Emmanuel, God with us, God for us, God in us, is the secret and the soul of spiritual progress.'

It was the divinity of man that the Master revealed — the true reality of man — in distinction from the degradation of man. This it was that he realized in himself, and that he pleaded with all men to realize in themselves.

It is a life foundation that will never have to shift its base in order to conform to an advancing knowledge or science. It is true to the best that our modern psychology is finding. If a child or a man is taught and believes that he is a worm of the dust, he will act as a worm of the dust. If he is taught, really taught, that he is a child of God, he will live and act as a child of God.

One of the greatest educators in the world's history, Froebel, built his entire educational system, as it is given in that great book, "The Education of Man," upon this truth.

In fact, the pith, the fundamental principle of his entire life, thought and teaching, is epitomized in his following brief state-ment: 'It is the destiny and life-work of all things to unfold their essence, hence their divine being, and, therefore, the Divine Unity itself — to reveal God in their external and transient being. It is the special destiny and life-work of man, as an intelligent and ra-tional being, to become fully, vividly, and clearly conscious of his essence, of the divine effluence in him, and, therefore, of God.'

The Master concerned himself but little with externals. He per-ceived and taught that the springs of life are all from within. As is the inner, therefore, so always will be the outer.

Therefore get right at the Centre, and life — the whole of life — will flow forth in an orderly and satisfactory manner. This is the natural and the normal way of living. Anything else is a perver-sion, and there is no satisfaction in it. Love that higher life, that life of God that is within you. Realize it as the Source of your life. And again I say, 'Seek ye first the Kingdom of God, and His righteousness; and all these things shall be added unto you.' And again I repeat, lest you forget, 'The Kingdom of God is within you.'

There is a definite law that operates here; otherwise there would be no truth in the Master's oft-repeated statement or injunction. His wonderful aptitude for discerning the things of the spirit, the fundamental laws of life, enabled him to apprehend it, to live it, to reveal and to teach it.

It is for us to know then that the Infinite Spirit of Life and Power illumines, and works in and through the individual life, when in our thought we become in tune with it, and realize it as the life and the power within us. The Infinite, the Central, power is always working; but we must definitely and consciously make contact with it in order that it may illumine, radiate, and work through us.

If the Master, with his wonderful insight and understanding, said, 'Of myself I can do nothing,' how can we expect, if we believe his word at all, to attain our highest unless we realize this same fact, and live likewise in the realization of the oneness of our life with the Father's life — the Divine rule, the Kingdom of God within us?

So essential, so fundamental is this, that some of his most striking parables are set forth to emphasize it, so that it will be made to grip out minds, and to sink into our consciences. The Kingdom of God is, in his mind, the one all-inclusive thing.

It is the pearl, he said, the pearl of great price. The merchant is seeking goodly pearls. He finds one of great value; and he goes immediately, sells all that he has, and buys it.

The Way that the Master taught is more a Way of Life than a religion. At the same time it is the very essence of religion, for the essence of all religion is the consciousness of God in the mind and the soul of man. It was this that he so clearly taught.

Reduced to its lowest and simplest terms, the Master's teaching might be stated: get right within, and all of your outward acts will then take care of themselves.

If we miss this great revelation of the Master — that to love God is to realize this inner Divine life within us, to open ourselves to it, and to live always under its guidance and its care; and its component part, that of love for the neighbour — we miss the very essence and heart of his revelation to the world.

We can hear him say: Love and live under the guidance of that higher life — the God life that is within you. When you do this you will realize it as the source of your neighbour's life — of all other men — therefore, all men are your brothers. Then kindness, sympathy, mutuality, co-operation, born of love, will be the guide and the watchword in all of your relations. And because this is the law of the universe, it will become the way of self-interest, as well.

Under this law of life and conduct will come the Kingdom of Heaven upon earth; but it comes in the lives of men and women first, then it blossoms and brings in the Kingdom of Heaven upon the earth. I have realized this, and now am revealing it unto you. If you believe what I say, and do as I say, then are you my disciples.

———————————

The religion of the Master is not subscribing to any beliefs, or any statement or formulated statements, about him. It is listening to him, and giving obedience when he says, 'Follow me.'

Try as we will, we cannot, if honest with ourselves, get away from his teaching of the Kingdom, that puts us in right relations, in tune, if you will, with the Centre of life — that for each man and each woman is within.

When a man finds this new, this real, Centre of life, by realizing his real relation with his God, he is brought, and automatically as it were, into right relations with his fellow men; and with this there comes a new motive into his life. Instead of striving as heretofore, working and gathering merely for himself — for his own little self alone and thereby missing happiness and satisfaction — he now becomes a co-worker with God, and in the service of his fellow men. Through this and this alone come happiness and satisfaction.

It is this new light, this new motive, that is animating increasing numbers of our men and women of great wealth and executive ability today. It is one of the notable characteristics of our time. Moreover, the vast amount of good that they are doing is wonderful. Some of them are becoming really great. The Master knew the law that is written deep in the universe when he said: 'He that is greatest among you, let him be your servant.'

And how much he had to say of love! And how definite and clear-cut were his statements.

'By this shall all men know that ye are my disciples, if ye have love one to another.'

That no one can live in hate and be a follower of the Christ is set forth as follows: 'If a man say, I love God, and hateth his brother, he is a liar: for he that loveth not his brother whom he hath seen, how can he love God whom he hath not seen?' And to his disciples he said: 'A new commandment I give you, That ye love one another; as I have loved you, that ye also love one another.' And notice the new spirit that he brings: 'Ye have heard that it hath been said, Thou shalt love thy neighbour, and hate thine enemy. But I say unto you, Love your enemies, bless them that curse you, do good to them that hate you, and pray for them which de-spitefully use you, and persecute you.'

He was so independent in his teaching — though sometimes teaching in the temple — that it incurred the enmity of the established ecclesiastical powers. It was revolutionary to them, who said that the proper access of man to God was through them, through their carefully constructed ecclesiastical system.

He was looked upon by them as a stirrer-up of the people. Moreover, his teachings were beginning to spread tremendously. He trod upon tradition, and in so doing he set at naught their self-claimed authority in religion.

It is valuable also to remember that the only people he ever really condemned were representatives of this very class. For the sinner he had always infinite pity and compassion, but not for them. Hear his words: 'Now do ye Pharisees make clean the outside of the cup and the platter; but your inward part is full of ravening and wickedness . . . . Woe unto you also, ye lawyers! for ye laden men with burdens grievous to be borne, and ye yourselves touch not the burdens with one of your fingers.'

This angered them the more, for they saw the danger of his truth to their institution and to themselves. They sought, and then devised a means to kill him, that they might, as they thought, check his truth. But he had brought a great truth into the world, and he would not be silenced.

He foresaw his fate, but he did not shrink from it. His vision and his knowledge of men were so great, that he realized and even said: 'And I, if I be lifted up from the earth, will draw all men unto me.' He understood so thoroughly the psychology of human nature.

He longed to escape the penalty; but he did not hesitate to give his life if need be as a ransom for the truth that he had perceived, and lived, and brought to the world. He was lifted up on a cross — for crucifixion was the regular Roman method of putting to death — but the same love that he lived and taught, he preserved to the end — 'Father, forgive them; for they know not what they do.' And finally — 'It is finished' — glad that the work that was given him to do was finished, and would, he felt, triumph.

The specific reasons, or rather 'charges,' the way he met them, the way that he seemed actually to court death and the way he met it, and what he said it meant to him, and his life message, will be dealt with briefly later.

So he was put to death by the Roman authorities, at the instigation of a little group of the Jewish hierarchy, who, entrenched in ecclesiastical power, fearing for their own authority and safety, were the worst enemies of their own and his own people. And we must never forget that Jesus, in common with all his disciples, lived, taught, and died a Jew.

He was put to death by this group, for which the Jewish people as a race should be held no more responsible than the American people should be held responsible for the death of Lincoln, because he met death through the conspiracy of a little group of Americans. Or again, any more than all of Christendom should be held responsible for the death of great numbers of the Master's true and loyal and equally brave followers, who, because they followed his teachings and lived his life as they understood them, were put to death by a similar hierarchy, who likewise feared for the institution and for their own authority and power.

The early Church of the Disciples was essentially a Jewish body. It was composed primarily of those who realized that the young Rabbi from Nazareth, whom they now acknowledged as their Master, had brought a new message of life, the life and the power of the Spirit, in distinction from a lifeless system of formalism. And it was the message of life that he brought, the message of a larger and a fuller life. This we must conclude if we catch the real spirit of his words: 'I am come that ye might have life, and that ye might have it more abundantly.'

It was clearly his initial and his consistent purpose to reveal God to man; in doing so he revealed man to himself. The established system of his day, as well as that which followed him, took man's pedigree from Adam. Jesus takes his pedigree from God. He realizes, as never man realized, the God, the Divine life within him. And then he taught that this is the real life of every man, and it is for all men to know and to realize it. Otherwise there would be but little meaning to his words: 'Call no man your father upon the earth: for one is your Father, which is in heaven.' Likewise to his words: 'As I am ye shall be.'

So in substance he says: If you are my disciple, my follower, you will follow me, and come into the realization of your life in the Father, and the same filial relations with the Father that I have come into.

All men, he taught, are sons of God; but the secret lies here — one must consciously and vividly realize this, and then live continually in this consciousness, in order that it may bring the guidance, the force, and the power into one's life that he said it would bring.

You must be born from above, his teaching said. This is the new birth, this consciousness of God in the soul. If it is real it will permeate and remould your entire life. Do this, and experience for yourself what a sense of direction and of power, what a sense of peace and joy and satisfaction comes to you.

. . . .My parable of the lost son shows you how empty and barren and unsatisfactory life becomes when it is lived purely in the external. The things that pertain to the body and the bodily senses alone, cannot satisfy. The real life lies deeper: It is to master and to rule the body and the things that pertain to it, and not to be mastered, or even enslaved by it; otherwise there are always heavy penalties to pay.

. . . .It is this that the younger son of my story, or parable, eventually finds to be true. When he finally comes to himself, and realizes the misery, the degradation of both mind and body that the purely sense life has brought him to, he longs then to go back to his father's house.

. . . .As soon as he forsakes his evil ways, the penalty of violated law ceases, and the father's forgiveness is instant. The estrangement is over, and love and forgiveness are of the very nature of the father. There are no sacrifices, no burnt offerings, no substitutions required. . . .

It is required simply to repent of our sins and errors, to realize our ignorant blunders, to turn from them, and to acknowledge and to give allegiance to that Divine life within, which will then assume the mastery, and which will raise life from the poor, mean, pitiable thing it so often is, to the high-born thing it not only can be but must be, in order to be happy and satisfactory.

It was truth that Jesus taught, not system. When we know the teachings of Jesus, in distinction from those about him, we find no system at all, much less any intricate system that bewilders or perplexes, that leads away from or obscures the fundamental truth that he taught, or that makes it more difficult to follow him.

So, The Way that Jesus taught — the religion if you like — is both Godward and manward. God is our father, and if Divine, then His divinity lives in us. We manifest our love for Him when we let the consciousness of this Divine life unfold and develop and dominate our lives. We then realize that this same life is the life in our fellows; and that when we know our real relation to them, it is that we are brothers.

And so there is no complex system, or anything that could possibly be called a system; that can truthfully be evolved from his twofold fundamental of love to God, and love for our fellow men. It is simply: love God, that Divine life within you; then the Spirit of truth, the Holy Spirit, will direct you and lead you. Do this, and then do not worry about your life. There is nothing to fear. Only trust.

As you do this, then faith and hope and courage grow and dominate, and become the creative and moulding forces in your life. Love your neighbour. Love him as friend and brother, for you are all children of the same father — partakers of the same Divine life.

Then is your life raised from that uncertain, fearing, doubting thing that it so often is, to one of trust and courage and conquering power.

To become centered in the Infinite, to go about our daily life and work, making contact with the very Source of wisdom and power, knowing that in God's life we are now living and there we shall live forever, above happenings and fears and forebodings, is the greatest gift that can come to any man, and this is the gift that the supreme Way-shower brought to the world.

Chapter 3
The Love and the Power of Life

Does my religion or what I term my religion depending upon whether or not it becomes a real vital creative force in my life—find its basis in the teaching of the Master that he so continually repeated, 'Seek ye first the Kingdom of God, and His righteousness; and all these things shall be added unto you' ? That there be no mistaking his meaning he likewise often said, 'Say not Lo here! or Lo there! for behold the Kingdom of God is within you.'

It is that Divine Centre within, from which every thought and every act in life must spring. It is the 'I am' of every man.

'Of myself I can do nothing,' he so often said. 'It is the Father that worketh in me; my Father works and I work.' Here undoubtedly is the true significance of the vitality of his statement: 'I and my Father are one.' Here undoubtedly is the true significance and vitality of his teaching:

'As I am you shall be.' Here undoubtedly is the truth of his teaching in regard to prayer that he so continually made use of, and so continually advised all others to make use of.

Advising against public prayer, for show or for its rhetorical effects, he enjoined: 'But thou, when thou prayest, enter into thy closet [that is, a place apart], and when thou hast shut thy door, pray to thy Father which is in secret; and thy Father which seeth in secret shall reward thee openly. Here undoubtedly lies the significance of his statement that he repeated so often in one form or another: 'According to your faith be it unto you.

Seek this Divine Centre of light, of truth, of illumination, and power—the God within you; Love and reverence and live in this realization and then, do not worry about your life.

God is Spirit, he taught, and Spirit is life. It is the One life, the universal source and spirit of life, manifesting in all individual expressions of life, in love, and direction, and power, and supply, in the degree that the individual rises to the consciousness, and lives in the consciousness, of that which is his life.

This again is unquestionably what Jesus meant when he said: 'I am come that you might have life, and that you might have it more abundantly.'

Each has life, but it is this more abundant life, this living in the vital consciousness of the life of God within, which is the thing that counts. It is this that culminates in a life lived to its full possibilities, and the joy that results from it. That the joy of life might be greater, might be full — he speaks of this so many times in one form or another.

The realization that this Divine Source, this Divine Centre of life, is within, cannot bring other than joy in life, but it must be realized and lived in. It must be the dominating love, and force, and guide. To long for it, to invite it, to believe and live in it, brings, and automatically, that more abundant and more joyous life.

He was always in dead earnest to help his fellow men, and went right down among those who needed help the most. No pious phrases, no institutionalism, no dogma, no peddling of any system — but help, real God-given human help.

With that wonderful inheritance, that wonderful and almost absolute aptitude for discerning the things of the mind and the spirit, with that keen but simple mind and heart, fired finally to the point of evangelism through an undoubtedly long and devoted period of preparation, he begins his memorable mission as a wandering teacher, by proclaiming to a little group out in the open in his own native Galilee: 'The time is fulfilled, and the Kingdom of God is at hand: repent ye, and believe the gospel. This and its amplification, often in simple, homely parable form, which all who heard him might understand, constituted the essence of his entire teaching.

The exhortations may have been like this: Repent means to turn. Gospel means good news; and so I call on you to turn and to hear the good news — that the Kingdom of God is at hand. The prophets before me and the teachers, even the most enlightened ones, have taught that Jehovah-God is above and overshadows his people. This is well, but I bring you something of more transcendent worth, something more vital - that God, the Father, lives within, and so guides, directs, and cares for His people. This is my realization, this I want to reveal to you. If you will not only hear my word, but believe and follow my word, you will experience a fuller, a richer, and a more joyous life.

. . . The time has come for an upward step in the evolution of human life. It comes through the knowledge that the spirit in man is one with the Spirit of life. The Spirit that has been believed as above and apart from man, is the life, the God-life that is in, and that is, the life of man.

. . . This is the Gospel, the good news, that I bring you. I have realized it myself. I reveal it to you, you who are dead in your trespasses and errors and sins — with the results that follow.

. . . Not realizing that larger source, that larger compass of life—the life of God within you— that larger illumining life of the Spirit, you have been living the sense-life only. But this is only a small portion, the more meager portion of life.

. . . The sense-life is of value, but it must be under the guidance and the domination of that higher life, the life of the Spirit. Otherwise there is many times the violation of law, spiritual law, mental law, physical law; and many times excesses that lead to suffering as all violation of law leads to suffering — and many times we do not know what is the matter with us.

. . . The sense-life is of great value, and can be made the source of much happiness and satisfaction. The five senses, the physical senses, relate us to the physical world in which we live. There would be no life here without them, but there is something in life infinitely beyond. It is creative Principle, it is the force of life that animates and that manifests itself in all form. It is the I Am that manifested itself to Moses, and that imparted to him greater understanding and power. It is the I Am of me, and the I Am of you. Some call it God. I call it — the Father. So I understand and so I live — The Father in me and I in the Father.

. . . This fills me with the love and power of life. It illumines, raises, and gives a higher realization of power in life. This I realize and, realizing it, I live always in the consciousness,

'It is the Father that worketh in me, my Father works and I work.' This I reveal to you, that your life may be raised to its higher values.

It is the realization of the Christ within. Christ is the universal divine nature in all. The Christ mind is the mind that realizes this. The Christ within is this unfolded consciousness, that in time becomes the centre from which the life in all of its details issues forth and is lived. This I have realized in my own life; this I impart to you.

. . . It is the pearl of great price. It is the greatest thing that can be known in life. It is the greatest possession that any man or woman can have. It is the one all-inclusive thing, for all good things in life follow in its train. Believe my words. Do this. Raise your thought, and thereby your life, up to this higher consciousness and then — do not be anxious about your life.

. . . This higher life of light and power impinges on the consciousness of every man and woman, just as it has on mine. It is through the channel of the mind that we must open ourselves that it may break through and illumine the soul, and give light and direction and power. This is that more abundant life which I would have you know and live. This is the very soul and heart and substance of my teaching.

If you do not believe me and reject it, you reject me, and I cannot be of the help to you that I long to be.

. . . Hear me. Hear my words. Don't reject this teaching of mine, this teaching of the Kingdom, this teaching of the life of God within. It will bring understanding to your mind, direction for your efforts and activities, supply for your needs and above all, perhaps, peace to your soul!

. . . It is indeed the new birth, that which I mean when I say: 'You must be born from above.' It is indeed as an earlier prophet said, 'Thou wilt keep him in perfect peace, whose mind is stayed on thee.' But we must use our minds as I tell you. We must open them to the truth and the guidance of this inner Kingdom, this Kingdom of God, this Kingdom of Heaven within. And that you may understand its importance, its all-inclusiveness — whereunto shall we liken it? Or with what comparison shall we compare it?

'The Kingdom of Heaven is like unto a grain of mustard seed, which a man took, and sowed in his field: which indeed is the least of all seeds; but when it is grown, it is the greatest among herbs, and becometh a tree, so that the birds of the air come and lodge in the branches thereof. (Matt. 13:31, 32)

'The Kingdom of Heaven is like unto leaven, which a woman took, and hid in three measures of meal, till the whole was leavened.' (Matt. 13:33)

'Again, the Kingdom of Heaven is like unto treasure hid in a field, the which when a man hath found, he hideth, and for joy thereof goeth and selleth all that he hath, and buyeth that held.' (Matt. 13:44)

How hard the Master tried to make the simple minds before him understand his message, and, understanding, appropriate it to their own lives and needs. No wonder that the common people heard him gladly — they whose minds had been stultified, they who had been befuddled and misled, they whose souls had been starved by the ecclesiastical leaders and dogmatists of their time, who had been giving them stones instead of bread.

No wonder that an awe and a longing and a new hope crept in and possessed them. No wonder there was a confidence inspired in them. No wonder they thought, 'Why, here is a man who speaks with authority.' No wonder they intuitively perceived the warmth and the truth of a real leader, one who had no personal motives, one who had a real love and a sense of real service for his fellows. No wonder that his fame spread abroad and that many followed him.

Chapter 4
The Days in the Little Carpenter's Shop

(AUTHOR'S NOTE: This chapter is of course purely imaginary. It may, however, have as much basis in truth as various other things that are in the accounts of the life of the Master.)

We would know more of Joseph, the father. He may have played a far more important part in the inheritance, and in the sympathetic companionship, of the eldest son than we know. The simple, homely type and manner of life and toiling together for their daily bread that there might be a supply for at least seven others would perchance suggest this.

Joshua, too, would perhaps have us help restore his well-nigh lost manhood — a loss which cripples his leadership among many clear-thinking and even devout men and women, and cripples therefore his big human-divine message, which to establish in the world was the absorbing passion of his life as well as the cause of his death.

It may help also his purpose (he who almost impatiently at times had to repeat, 'I am a man as you are'), which institutionalism has well-nigh emasculated and frustrated.

No wonder the people said: Our teachers have not this man's manner — the manner of this man Jesus. They are continually harping on, 'It is said,' 'The prophets have said.' But there is no life in their words. And besides, they impose upon us such silly practices and observances and mumbling formulas.

The things they give us sink as stones in our stomachs, while this man truly gives us bread to eat; and besides, his very teaching makes him brave.

Ezra, Ezra Ben Joseph, was over in the adjoining village yesterday. He heard Jesus there, and what do you think he said? (Come close and do not repeat it. Say not that I told you.)

Right in the face of two who were there — he was speaking of the priesthood of his and our religion and the traditions of its priests and elders — he said: 'Woe to you, scribes and Pharisees, hypocrites! for you take tithes on mint, dill and cumin, and have overlooked the more important matters of the law, such as justice, mercy, and trustworthiness; which were necessary for you to have done, and by no means to have left undone. . . . Oh, blind guides, who strain at gnats and swallow camels.'

The Romans oppress us and rob us — damn their souls. (Come closer.) God knows we have little enough; but these that this Jesus denounces as hypocrites, that sit in the high seats and mumble their self-made formulas, and imprecations, and penalties, arrayed in their fine robes which they collect the pence from us to pay for, do us the greater harm. Woe to us! Woe to us, and to our children!

Let us arise and follow him, this man Jesus. Surely he is a teacher sent of God. Some do not believe in him because he is a Nazarene. They say, 'What good can come out of Nazareth, that small village less than twenty furlongs from us!' At Nazareth he was known as Joshua Ben Joseph. His father had a carpenter's shop there that joined on to their home.

My father worked at one time with Joseph in his shop. He was an older man, but always kindly and thoughtful. While my father was there Joshua Ben Joseph and his next younger brother worked also in the shop. There were five brothers: Joshua the older, and James, and Joses, and Jude, and Simon. There were two or three sisters — two that my father met, but he never learned their names. Joshua as a young man, my father said, when he worked with him in the shop at Nazareth, had a strong, vigorous constitution, and always a happy, buoyant disposition. He was always thoughtful, but always pleasant to work with. He was a good worker and always helpful to any working with him.

He and his father Joseph always got along well together, and there seemed to be an unusual comradeship between them. They would joke with each other and seemed always happy to be together, and this seemed to lighten their work in the shop.

My father told of an incident that occurred while he was working there: a woman came into the shop to have some work done. She was the wife of the Rabbi of the little synagogue at Nazareth. She argued long and hot with Joseph to make him do the job at a much lower price than he was willing to contract to do it for.

Joseph stood his ground, and she went out to another shop. When she had gone Joseph sat down on the bench as if to get a bit of rest from the ordeal, and said to Joshua: 'Look at that! She has taken almost an hour of my time, trying to get her work done at about one half of what it is worth; and they have a great deal more money than we have. In a good-humoured way Joshua replied: 'Well, father, you shouldn't belong to the same race.'

'Anyway,' replied Joseph, 'I hope she will stick to the Gentile shop she has gone to, and that her shadow will never darken the door of this shop again.'

'Come now, father, enjoined Joshua, laughing, 'she's the Rabbi's hurmat. [a husband's most sacred possession].

Joseph, with a twinkle in his eye, replied, 'But not entirely jubn, [shy, retiring, of few words], and got up and went to work again.

While Joshua was a good worker, he seemed always when his work was done to want to be alone — either alone or down at the caravanserai when the caravans came in, especially those from Egypt and India. When he returned one evening from the caravanserai my father overheard, through the little window, part of a conversation with his mother in regard to Gautama Siddhartha and his followers — and his longing to know more of the real teaching of the Buddha.

He repeated then something that he had heard which Gautama Siddhartha had said as a young man and after long periods of contemplation and thought: 'I have awakened to the truth, and I am resolved to accomplish my purpose — verily I shall become a Buddha.' It was this deep conviction and resolve that made him become the Light-bearer to vast millions of people. 'My people,' continued Joshua, 'need help. It would be a wonderful thing to be the Way-shower to my people. How they need a deliverer!' Then he added, 'Tomorrow there will be no work in the shop, and I will go early to the mountain for the day, that I may know more of my Father's love and purpose, and business.'

There was a gentle reminder and remonstrance on the part of the mother then, about his going with them to the synagogue, that he might hear the reading and the expounding of the Scripture, and - 'lest the neighbours talk.'

Joshua listened very attentively and then said: 'I love the Law and the Prophets, the religion of my Fathers. I honour those men of God, and I get from them all that I can; but today is a new day. God has given me a heart for longing, as well as for reverence. He has given me a mind to use, and a leading to follow, and He will hold me responsible for the way I use that mind, and the way I follow that leading.

'If my heart is pure and my longing is great, He will reveal Himself to me in the unfolding light, and the duty of today. The manna that He gave to our people in the wilderness in caring for their needs was for the day that He gave it; stored and hoarded it staled and rotted. His promise was more for the new day. They trusted him, and the new day's supply never failed them.

'There is no such thing as "the truth once delivered." That is a shameful lie, intended to palliate and deceive the people. And if they are slow enough mentally, and cowardly enough morally, to believe it, they are the ones who must suffer, but suffer they must. It is the law of God and from it there is no escape.

'Because of our moral cowardice, and our mental lethargy, a priesthood has established itself in our religion. They repeat over and over again, "It is said," "The prophets have said." A dead level has ensued, and no prophet has arisen to speak to us for over three hundred years.

'The prophet thinks and aspires and listens. He goes to the mountain for his message. God meets him in this High Place of communion; and depending upon his aspirations, his motives, and his faith, he speaks audibly or inaudibly, marking the difference between the greater or the lesser prophet.

'In either case, then, he comes down from the High Place, he gives his message and leads the people for a while. Then he goes, and sooner or later — and it is surprising sometimes how soon — the priest sets about modifying the faith, fashions it into a system, builds a dogma and an organization upon it, and guarding it as his own in this form, makes his living upon it. Many times, then, he with others fashions it into a high-towering system for personal and political power. The motive is self — as it rides the backs of the people.

'That is what has happened to all religions, and what should be the life-giving and helpful has become lifeless, stale, and in some cases rotten. Blind leaders of the blind! The condition of our people is pitiable. They are as sheep straying without a shepherd. They need deliverance from their overlords, the Romans, but more than this they need deliverance from the more deadly overlords, the priests and the scribes. As the great prophet-singer said: "Where there is no vision, the people perish."

'A deliverer must come. God's light, as He reveals it today, must illumine and energize a Messiah, one accepted and anointed of God to give today's truth, and through it life and light and power to carry on, to the people.

'Don't think that I am a fanatic, mother, or that I am beside myself; also forgive me if I seem to speak harshly of the religion of your people. Whether with your consent or without your consent — but I hope with your blessing — I must go to the mountain tomorrow, and often. I have established relations with God, my

Father, there, and I must be alert and obedient and carry them through. And I foresee the time, mother — do not grieve or be anxious when I must leave my father Joseph's shop, to be about my Father's business — my real Father's.

'I have talked it over with my father Joseph, as we have worked long days together in the shop. He understands. The work has been at times hard, but we have always got along well together. It was only yesterday that he said: "You have been more than an obedient son to your mother and to me. I have had a responsibility — nine of us to care for, and work not always plentiful. Our little carpenter's shop has had its ups and its downs as you know, but you have helped lighten my load. James and Joses are growing up and they can take your place. When you go you will go with my blessing, as well as my gratitude.

"'I am proud of you, my son. I appreciate the help that you have been, the confidence that you have had in me, and I in you. I am grateful for the good times we have had together. I believe you will prove a teacher, a prophet, truly chosen of God. My God and your God will care for you, as He always has cared for us.

"He will care for you in the degree that you make His business your business. But this I have never told you, and I hesitate to tell you now: I shudder to think what may in time be in store for you. Ignorance, and passion, and blind leadership on the part of the people, combined with self-seeking, jealous ecclesiasticism and fury, have combined to kill some of our greatest prophets — God help and protect you. But one were a coward to stifle oneself, and not go forward. I may not live to see it, I must go down — you must go up.

"'Each must live his own life according to his light. God raises up the light-bearer, the Way-shower, when he is sorely needed. Our people are in sore need. I rejoice to see your day. You have been candid and open in unfolding yourself to me. You have helped me, and I know full well what you mean by your real Father, and your Father's business. I do not resent it.

"'Some of your brothers and sisters have smiled and have talked. Some of the neighbours have talked, but that is always so. Your mother sometimes questions, and doesn't seem always to know. That is many times true. Our real relations are not always those of our own household. They are those who are most akin to us in mind and sympathy and spirit — many times they are not related to us by blood ties. It would save many a heartache and misunderstanding did people realize this law more fully.

"'Your mother's mother, Ann — who is one of the salt of the earth — understands you, and stands up for you, and it is by virtue of her understanding and her sympathy that you have always thought so much of her. She divines the part that you will play with our people.

"'Do you ever recall when you were a little boy? I do often. Every weekend you would take her that big bag of shavings which we would fill here together in the shop. I can see you yet as you trudged up the hill — such a little boy and such a big bag on your back.

"'She lived alone then in her well-kept little house, and she was always on the look-out for your coming. Pushing open the door she would say: 'Here is little Joshua, my saviour. My fire will glow now brightly again; and it will be so much easier for me that he has come with his cheery smile, and his big bag of shavings. And how clean they smell — just like Joseph's shop.'

"'I think she looked forward every week to your coming, and staying to have the evening meal with her on that day. She would always have the farthing ready for you. You would say:

'No, grandma, I didn't bring the shavings for hire, I brought the shavings for you.'

"''Bless you, little Joshua,' she would say, 'I know you did, but the labourer is always worthy of his hire.' She had imagination. She understood the child mind and heart. She had sympathy, sympathy that makes the world kin. That was the reason you were always so fond of her, and so was I and all who knew her.'"

Chapter 5
He Called it 'The Way'

The Way of the Master is indeed a wonderful way if we will but understand what he meant. God is love, he taught, and love is the very essence of God. God to him was Father, the term that he so continually uses. The Father cares for him and reveals Himself to him, because he seeks to know and to do, and in doing reveals the Father's will.

He trusts the Father, and the Father enlightens him. He trusts the Father, and the Father cares for him. Through his mind in the attitude of desire and trust, he lives in a filial relationship with the Father, and the Father responds to his every desire and need.

My Father who loves me and cares for me, is your Father who loves you and cares for you. It is for all men to realize this and come into the same filial relationship with the Father. Life is hard and uncertain, filled with fears and forebodings. It should not be so. It is not the natural order of life. Instead of being estranged from God, we should draw nigh to God. God rules in the world and on the earth, and replenishes the earth, but always through established laws. God lives and rules in the life of man; but He does this through the channel of man's mind. This is the law - the established law.

The things we see and feel get their being, in form, from the creative force that is their mainspring. It is the creative force which man calls God that gives form to his body and that shapes his world — his individual world. Were it withdrawn, or were anything to interfere sufficiently with its functioning, the body would become an inert mass, dead, as we say, and likewise his individual world. So the life of individual man, the individual tributary, opens out into the great sea of life, which is its source.

To know that the individual life and its Power are one with the Infinite Spirit of life and power, enlarges one's consciousness and gives a larger reception from the Source for that life. It was the flood-gate of this larger reservoir of life that, with his supreme aptitude for discerning the things of the mind and the spirit, the Master opened; and it so flooded his own understanding of life, that it pushed him out as a revealer of this larger truth of life to all who would hear and believe his word. It was a great intuitive perception or consciousness which opened the knowledge of this life to the Way-shower.

Speaking of this larger life, and of Jesus who perceived and who revealed it so completely, it was that highly illumined philosopher, Fichte, who said: 'An insight into the absolute unity of the human existence with the Divine is certainly the profoundest knowledge that man can attain. . . . Jesus of Nazareth undoubtedly possessed the highest perception containing the foundation of all other truth, of the absolute identity of humanity with the Godhead, as regards what is essentially real in the former.'

And how clear-cut and, coming from such a source, how convincing is his thought in his conclusion: 'From the first standing-point the Eternal Word becomes flesh, assumes a personal, sensible, and human existence, without obstruction or reserve, in all times, and in every individual man who has a living insight into his unity with God, and who actually and in truth gives up his personal life to the Divine Life within him — precisely in the same way as it became incarnate in Jesus.'

Significant also in this same connection are these words of Swedenborg, that highly gifted scientist and seer: 'There is only one Fountain of life, and the life of man is a stream therefrom, which, if it were not continually replenished from its source, would instantly cease to flow. . . . Every created thing is in itself inanimate and dead, but it is animated and caused to live by this, that the Divine is in it and that it exists in and from the Divine.'

Kindred in his thought is that of the beloved philosopher, Rudolf Eucken, late of Jena. Whenever he deals with Christianity he makes it plain that it is this alive and vital Christianity of the Way-shower, the Christ of Galilee, in distinction from the Christianity of the creeds and dogmas of the past. To a purport almost identical with the fundamental thought of Fichte — that the Divine Life and energy actually lives in us, is inseparable from religion — Eucken has said: 'Religion is not merely a belief in some supreme Power, nor do I consider it to be the establishment of relations of any kind between this supreme Power and ourselves. It is an inner identification with it and the creation of a new life through it. . . . The union of the Divine and human nature is the fundamental truth of religion, and its deepest mystery consists in the fact that the Divine enters into the compass of the Human without impairing its Divinity. With this new phase, life is completely renewed and elevated. Man becomes immediately conscious of the infinite and eternal, of that within him which transcends the world. For the first time the love of God becomes the ruling motive of his life, and brings him into an inner relation with the whole scope of reality. . . . It is here that we find a new self, our true spiritual self.

'The cleavage in the depth of our souls is bridged over at last. That inner estrangement, so often felt, has disappeared and the whole universe is now part of regenerate man's experience. That feeling of isolation disappears, which so often depressed us, and we are conscious of partaking in that "inner life" common to all of us. I cannot conceive of the development of a powerful personality, a deep-rooted and profound mind, or a character rising above this world, without his having experienced this divine life. . . . That is what I believe to be the character of Christianity.'

Emerson epitomizes his conclusion in regard to the Master in brief and clear-cut form: 'Alone in all history he estimated the greatness of man. One man was true to what is in me and you. He saw that God incarnates Himself in man, and ever more goes forth anew to take possession of the world.'

All of the men just quoted were staunch seekers after and revealers of truth, free and independent in their thought. No one of them was the representative of any system or institution or dogma, and that is one of the chief reasons why they all stand so high in the estimation of thinking men and women everywhere. That is why their thought is of real value in light and help.

Seeking for truth with unbiased minds, they found it in simple clear-cut form, and gave it expression in similar form. Their reception and understanding of truth were, on the one hand, similar to those of Jesus. On the other hand, their finding and understanding of Jesus were no part of any perplexing or mystifying system that he himself would so thoroughly condemn, even as he condemned the self-seeking purveyors of system woven around and strangling the truth of the prophets before him.

So deeply was his righteous soul stirred by the system that he found in vogue in his time, giving stones for bread, empty formulas instead of truth — for power, or self-show, or money — that he did not restrain himself.

Speaking in very articulate form, either of or to the expounders of ecclesiastical system and form, he said: 'Woe unto you, lawyers! for ye have taken away the key of knowledge: ye entered not in yourselves, and them that were entering in ye hindered.' And again: 'Woe unto you, scribes and Pharisees, hypocrites! for ye compass sea and land to make one proselyte, and when he is

made, ye make him twofold more the child of hell than yourselves.'
'Ye are as graves which appear not, and the men that walk over
them are not aware of them.'

Search as we will, we shall find that it was the burning purpose
of Jesus to make lighter the burdens of common men and women,
who had their doubts to face, their problems to meet, their battles
to fight, their fears to conquer. This he did in simple common
language by showing them primarily that there was nothing to be
afraid of — nothing except their doubts and their fears. But how?
how? — as is the cry of common men today — How? How?

He proclaimed and taught this on that opening day of his ministry: through the gift of the truth, the truth that had been revealed
to him, and that he longed to reveal to others; the truth that, if
they would but believe him, would become the veritable gift of God
to them. With this high purpose and with his high faith he proclaimed his ministry: 'The time is fulfilled, and the Kingdom of God
is at hand: repent ye, and believe the gospel.' Repent — turn, and
believe the gospel — the good news.

The good news is what I mean when I say: You shall know the
truth and the truth shall make you free. It is the knowledge of God
the knowledge that God, whom you have been worshipping as afar
off, is within you. He is the life, the Spirit of life within you — the
Infinite Spirit of life and power that is behind all, working in and
through all, the life of all the life therefore in you.

When you realize this you will find that you are not alone; and
the more fully you realize this, the more fully you will find yourself
conscious of an enlarging reception of life and light and energy
and power. You are born in the sense consciousness with all of
the sense limitations. I bring you knowledge of a higher consciousness, which is the consciousness of the spirit, the spirit of God
within you. You must be born anew — you must be born from
above; and this new birth opens up, and makes active in your life,
possibilities and powers that otherwise lie dormant and dead.

It becomes in you a fountain of life, watering the soil for an ever-
greater harvest in your life. It reveals the Christ within you, and
makes you heir, joint heir of God. It lights your way and it lightens
your burden, for then: you realize and live in the consciousness:
It is the Father that worketh in me, my Father works and I work.

It is the nature of the Father to give good gifts unto His children.
You must have faith, and as is your faith, so will be your realization and your life.

'Ask, and it shall be given you; seek, and ye shall find; knock, and it shall be opened unto you: for every one that asketh receiveth; and he that seeketh findeth; and to him that knocketh it shall be opened. Or what man is there of you, whom if his son ask bread, will he give him a stone? Or if he ask a fish, will he give him a serpent? If ye then, being evil, know how to give good gifts unto your children, how much more shall your Father which is in heaven give good things to them that ask him? Therefore all things whatsoever ye would that men should do to you, do ye even so to them: for this is the law and the prophets.' (Matt. 7:7-12)

The eye of faith then becomes clearer in its vision through the guidance of the spirit, the spirit within.

'The light of the body is the eye: if therefore thine eye be single, thy whole body shall be full of light. But if thine eye be evil, thy whole body shall be full of darkness. If therefore the light that is in thee be darkness, how great is that darkness!' (Matt. 6:22, 23)

This higher conception of life which the Master realized and taught — that we should under this higher guidance with implicit and without fear or foreboding — he called The Way. It seems to our sort of earth-bound, led, material type of thought almost unbelievable; but he said it was true. It was to him so plain, and he spoke with such absolute knowledge of it, that he called it the 'pearl of great price,' this knowledge of the Kingdom and the power of God within.

It is for each individual to be wise enough to make it the predominating reality, and therefore the source of the greatest good in his life. To open oneself to this inner Power and to live continually under its guidance — and then to go about one's work with faith, with full implicit faith, was his injunction.

'Therefore I say unto you, Take no thought for your life, what ye shall eat, or what ye shall drink; nor yet for your body, what ye shall put on. Is not the life more than meat, and the body than raiment? Behold the fowls of the air: for they sow not, neither do they reap, nor gather into barns; yet your heavenly Father feedeth them. Are ye not much better than they? Which of you by taking thought can add one cubit unto his stature? And why take ye thought for raiment? Consider the lilies of the field, how they grow; they toil not, neither do they spin: and yet I say unto you, That even Solomon in all his glory was not arrayed like one of these. Wherefore, if God so clothe the grass of the field, which today is, and tomorrow is cast into the oven, shall he not much more clothe you, O ye of little faith? Therefore take no thought, saying, What shall we eat? or, What shall we drink? or, Wherewithal shall we be

clothed? (For after all these things do the Gentiles seek:) for your
heavenly Father knoweth that ye have need of all these things. But
seek ye first the Kingdom of God, and his righteousness; and all
these things shall be added unto you.' (Mate. 6:25-33)

It seems a wonderful way of life, but he knew. A help, a great help
lies here: To follow this teaching of the Master, by living always in
the realization of this Kingdom within, and then to go about one's
daily work thinking or voicing, but always living and resting in: Be
still — And know — I am — God.

> Be still
> And know
> I am
> God.

Give God the chance. 'According to your faith be it unto you.' He
knew, and the purpose, the great passion, of his life was that all
other men might know.

Chapter 6
To Know That All is Well

Although The Way of the Master seems to be a wonderful way, it should unquestionably be the natural and normal life for every man. Life would not be so complex if we did not so persistently make it so. To resolve absolutely to cut loose from fear, which inhibits the higher power within us, which clouds our vision, which neutralizes our efforts, and brings desolation and ruin to many a life, would mark the beginning of a new life for many.

To live in this higher consciousness, to enthrone faith and hope and courage, is to give way to a positive creative type of thought that clarifies the way, strengthens the spirit, and that all the time is working out the thing, the desired end, along the lines that we are going.

Thought is a force, and its invariable law is that like creates like, and that the life always and invariably follows the thought. As we think, we become, and the glory of life is that it is given to each to be the master of his thought.

Faith is of this type of thought — this positive building type of thought. Belief, in the sense that the Master so often used the word, is of this same type of thought, and the basis of his saying — If thou canst but believe, all things are possible to him that believes. To live in this higher consciousness where the thought is always under the guidance of the spirit, and then to go about one's work each day, knowing that all is well, projects not only a power but a happiness into life, which is a part of The Way.

An earlier prophet glimpsed somewhat the truth that the Master realized and revealed so completely when he said: 'And thine ears shall hear a word behind thee, saying, This is the way, walk ye in it, when ye turn to the right hand, and when ye turn to the left.'

Emerson, speaking our Western language, said: 'Man is not only the inlet but he may become the outlet of all there is in God.' In saying this he was in substantial agreement with the prophet, and with the Master.

Yes, there is a reality, a directing power that will not fail us, if we will but trust ourselves to it, if we will do our part. It is through the channel of the mind that we must do our part, in both an active and a receptive form.

Said that great industrialist, Henry Ford, who, sensitively organized, has a contact with something somewhere which the ordinary man doesn't have and which to my mind accounts for his ability to see ahead of the other fellow and to project things on a large scale: 'We are central stations with myriads of entities going and coming all the time with messages. Thus no one is alone, no one is helpless. All the material and insight that exists is available for those who send for it and can use it. The more you use the more you have. One of the cardinal rules of life is use. If you want more of anything, use what you have.'

Our conversation had been about the inner powers and forces, and I then made bold to put to him the question: 'You feel, do you, that if thought is a force — as we must recognize it is — there is such a thing as cultivating it in some way, so that we may use it more effectively than we ordinarily do — say, by way of some definite direction of it, by concentration?'

His answer was: 'Intensify your thought and you set up attraction. Concentrate on a job, and you attract all the things necessary to accomplish it. You attract the things you give a great deal of thought to. I have had to quit many jobs and wait because I haven't spent enough thought on them. I have had to wait for certain things to come around. . . . You attract what you need by putting a lot of thought on it, then all the necessary elements or entities come round where you can use them. A thing will build itself up if you keep your thought on it. Thoughts are materials.'

It is interesting, almost amazing and truly gratifying, to find by talking with them how large is the number of men of affairs, big affairs along one line or another, who are alive to these truths, who are studying them and pursuing them, who are interested in the laws of these inner powers and forces of life, and who are using them in their lives.

Many of them are men, moreover, who, recognizing their universality, and their universality as the common denominator in human life, are using their means and their abilities for the common good. It gives one great hope for the future. It makes one feel that there will come a balance to the more mechanistic conception of life — the saving power in this our so-called machine age.

They are realizing that these bigger and more real things in life, the things of the mind and the spirit, together with the realization of the oneness of all life, pay, after all, the larger dividends, and bring the real and abiding pleasures and satisfactions in life.

May I digress for a moment to mention an occurrence which suggests itself here? Some years ago it was my pleasure to stay in Michigan for a little visit with a friend who when he died some time later left a fortune of many million dollars. Inheriting nothing but a good mind and a good native ability, he had made a modest fortune. His health broke and he lost it all. After the restoration of his health several years before my visit, he had commenced again to build a fortune that he started on his kitchen stove.

He was a man of rare vision and patience. Tall and of splendid physique when I knew him, he told me he was but skin and bones, as the saying goes, when he started his way back to health again. Exhausting the skill of doctors and specialists and sanatoriums, even in the summer weather he was encased in three suits of underclothing and an overcoat, moving here and there in his wheelchair.

One day in conversing with a friend, he was told of a little woman in the same city who had accomplished some remarkable things in the realm of healing. He was seized with a strong conviction, and had himself wheeled to her little cottage. Describing his condition, and his futile efforts in regaining his health, he told her that he had come to stay with her. 'But,' she protested, 'I have no room for you. I can't take you.' 'That's all right,' he replied, 'but I am here, and I am here to stay. Seeing his determination, she found a way. To explain the situation he said to me:

'I realized in the presence of this little woman that she had something that I, with my business and executive ability, had not got. He then set forth in a graphic way how at the very first treatment he could feel the quickening and the warming of his blood as in a vitalized form it coursed through his system. He became interested in the things she knew. This interest grew, and he began to make a careful study of the inner powers and forces of life, which he pursued with increasing ardour as the years passed. He was practically healed, he said, when he left the little cottage, and he left it with a far greater knowledge of life than when he was wheeled into it.

He then began to make a study of foods, an intensive study; for he felt that the preservation of health, which is the chief value in life, was dependent to a very great extent upon the food we eat. The blood stream is the very fountain of life, of the bodily life, externalizing in the body always of its kind; and the right elements in food must be supplied to manufacture a vital and healthy type of blood.

He became convinced that what is the matter with the great pro-
portion of people with whom something is the matter is defective
eating, primarily the eating of too much denatured food, as well as
unwise combinations of food, and in many cases over-eating, with
under-exercise. This, combined with his own recent experience of
the influence of the mind and the spirit on the body, gave him a
knowledge of health that he had never had before, and enabled
him eventually to be of great help in this realm to many people.

But getting back to the primary purpose of relating this anec-
dote: My friend had purchased some acres of ground adjoining
his factories on which he had built a number of very attrac-
tive cottages, each with an adequate parcel of ground. These he
sold to his workers at practically the cost of construction on liberal
terms of payment. A little beyond them, he had built a simple cottage for himself — and for quiet. When the cares of the growing
business and his contact with people began to get him away from
his bearings, he would go there sometimes for a couple of days at
a time, to be entirely alone, for rest, for thought, for meditation,
and recreation. He recalled how necessary he found this in order
to preserve the right balance in life, to keep himself up to par, that
he might the more fully enjoy life.

It is an interesting bit of human experience, and it carries a lesson for all. Life is more than food and drink, more than business,
more than money. Business and money are a means to an end,
like riches, but never an end in themselves.

And before leaving the matter — the little woman! She had sat at
the feet of the Master, and she believed his Word. With a natural
interest, and evidently with an unusual aptitude in herself, she
was impressed with his acts of healing. She heard him repeat so
many times, 'Believest thou that I can do this thing?' and the answer being always in the affirmative, she heard him, 'According to
thy faith be it unto thee: Be thou whole.'

She then realized that to heal, or to be of help in the healing of
another, it is necessary, through the genuineness and the power
of one's own life, to instill a confidence in that other sufficient to
arouse his subconscious mind to such a degree of activity that a
subtle force is engendered, which produces the healing.

With so much physical suffering in the world, so many distraught
minds and nerves, and so many ill bodies, there are many who
have wondered, many who still wonder, why the Church has so
completely forgotten or even repudiated the example and indeed
the direct command of the Master. After instructing his disciples

and apostles and demonstrating to them, he commissioned them, as they went out to spread his gospel and his message, also to render a healing service — 'He sent them to preach the Kingdom of God, and to heal the sick.'

But on second thoughts, and when we know the history of what transpired later on, why this occurred becomes clear, and will be considered more fully later. It was a part, and a very important part, in the life of the little congregations that began to take form here and there, wherever his disciples went. The Master was always keenly alive to every form of human need, and we cannot help believing from the meager accounts of his life we have, that he intentionally made the alleviation of human suffering, which took so many forms in his day, a very real portion of his ministry.

There are individuals, and there are various groups, at whose hands it is finding a revival, and in some cases a very significant and vital revival, among his followers of today, in our own and in many other countries.

Chapter 7
That Superb Teaching of SIN

The Palestinian Jew of Jesus' day had not only a very limited knowledge of the world and its extent, as we know it now, but an exceedingly limited knowledge of the facts and the laws of the universe — the laws of nature, and the laws pertaining to and governing human life, as we know them now.

The matter of sin, and its consequences and penalties, occupied an important place in the thoughts and minds of the people. God was not only a punisher of sin — the sins of His, the 'chosen people' — but was also always on the look-out to punish the sins of the individual. He demanded appeasement of His wrath, so they thought, and in this thought they acted.

Offerings to purchase appeasement, and forgiveness, and cleansing, were made. A system had been manufactured for them, and accepted on the part of many, whereby burnt offerings of slain animals, or parts of them, were burned on the altar of forgiveness, as a propitiation for their sins.

Sin bulked large in the minds of these early people, as it did in that intricately established system which took form from three to four hundred years after Jesus' time, and which, pushing far into the background his message and teachings to the extent of almost completely ignoring them, concerned itself with intricate discussions of things, speculative things about him.

Both systems now seem non-essential or even puerile, though they have a certain interesting historical value to thinking men and women of today; and to be honest one should add, to devout men and women of today. They believe that the Infinite creative power, or if we prefer the term, God, works always through well-established laws — laws that it is given to men to find, to formulate, and to observe.

They believe that God does not punish, as we ordinarily understand the term. The violation of the law in itself carries its own punishment, and its observance carries its own reward. The violation of law, either intentionally or unwittingly, be it a law of the universe in which we live, or a law of human living or conduct, brings its corresponding punishment.

To observe and to live in harmony with the laws of the universe about us and with the laws of human living and conduct, brings always beneficent results. The observance of law, then, brings good and always good to him who has intelligence enough to understand and to know it, and sense and will enough to obey it.

The violation of law carries always and inevitably its punishment and penalties in the form of suffering and loss. No man has ever been able enough or keen enough, and no man probably ever will be, to escape such penalty and punishment. Better, then, to use one's wits and one's will to know and obey the law. The moment the violation ceases, that moment the penalty ceases, and the suffering and the loss which have been its demand begin to decrease and will finally disappear.

God then does not punish except through the laws that are already decreed. God is not a book-keeper, but a life-giver, a creator, an establisher of laws. Wise, then, is he who when he stumbles or falls does not waste time in bemoaning his fate, but picks himself up, and all the better instantly, gives himself time to see and to understand the cause of the stumble or the fall with its resultant pain or suffering or loss, and goes on about his work with the cheery determination — never again.

To waste time and energy in regret, which but weakens an otherwise determined spirit, is infinitely worse than to learn and to take to heart in a determined manner, even a joyous manner, a lesson in experience.

The word translated sin in our Scripture means, literally, a missing of the mark, of the goal — as applied to the runner in a race, the participant in a game. The management doesn't set penalties for him who fails in the race or the game, doesn't kill him, doesn't demand any satisfaction that he or someone else must pay. It is simply that the award is withheld from him. It is given to the one who knows the rules of the game, and who plays the game, better than he.

When the races or the games occur again, he, with the experience he has gained, with better knowledge of the rules, and with a more enlightened and determined practice, has still an equal chance to win. If he has stamina and backbone, and is willing to pay the price in practice, intelligent practice, and if he has a high-born determination and courage, he probably will win. It depends on whether he is able to change 'can' to 'will.'

He may take a leaf from Vergil, who gave to the world enlightening precepts a hundred years or so before Jesus' time and who said, describing the crew that to his mind would win the race: 'They can because they think they can.'

The Master was far more interested in instilling faith and hope and courage in the minds and hearts of his hearers through deeper and better understanding of life, than he was in recalling to them their sins, or indeed in saying very much to them about their sins.

His insight, his knowledge of life and of human nature, led him to deal always with the positives rather than the negatives of life. His teachings were always creative, constructive, life-giving; not deadening, paralyzing, defeative.

He knew the tragedy that creeps into innumerable lives, into minds weak enough and morally flabby enough to go through life continually bowed down with a sense of sin, rather than strong enough quickly to make restitution if it be a sin against the neighbour, or to stop the violation of law through a common-sense use of mind and will, if it be otherwise.

One of the most significant things in his entire ministry is his incomparable parable of the so-called lost, or prodigal, son. It is perhaps the world's supreme conception and teaching — or shall we say elucidation? — of what we term sin and the sinner, and how masterfully it is put!

It would seem that no complex system, built upon a deliberate departure from the teaching of the Master, and the formulation of a metaphysical substitution about him, could ever take place. Not condemnation, but consideration and love, is the very essence of the Father's nature.

'A certain man had two sons: and the younger of them said to his father, "Father, give me the portion of goods that falleth to me." And he divided unto them his living. And not many days after the younger son gathered all together, and took his journey into a far country, and there wasted his substance with riotous living. And when he had spent all, there arose a mighty famine in that land; and he began to be in want. And he went and joined himself to a citizen of that country; and he sent him into his fields to feed swine. And he would fain have filled his belly with the husks that the swine did eat: and no man gave unto him. And when he came to himself, he said, How many hired servants of my father's have bread enough and to spare, and I perish with hunger! I will arise and go to my father, and will say unto him, Father, I have sinned against heaven, and before thee, and am no more worthy to be called thy son: make me as one of thy hired servants.

'And he arose, and came to his father. But when he was yet a great way off, his father saw him, and had compassion, and ran, and fell on his neck, and kissed him. And the son said unto him, Father, I have sinned against heaven, and in thy sight, and am no more worthy to be called thy son. But the father said to his servants, Bring forth the best robe, and put it on him; and put a ring on his hand, and shoes on his feet: And bring hither the fatted calf, and kill it; and let us eat, and be merry: for this my son was dead, and is alive again; he was lost, and is found. And they began to be merry.

'Now his elder son was in the field: and as he came and drew nigh to the house, he heard music and dancing. And he called one of the servants, and asked what these things meant. And he said unto him, Thy brother is come; and thy father hath killed a fatted calf, because he hath received him safe and sound. And he was angry, and would not go in: therefore came his father out, and entreated him. And he answering said to his father, Lo, these many years do I serve thee, neither transgressed I at any time thy commandment; and yet thou never gavest me a kid, that I might make merry with my friends: but as soon as this thy son was come, which hath devoured thy living with harlots, thou hast killed for him the fatted calf. And he said unto him, Son, thou art ever with me, and all that I have is thine. It was meet that we should make merry, and be glad: for this thy brother was dead, and is alive again; and was lost, and is found.' (Luke 15:11-32)

It is indeed a wonderful parable, from the standpoint of the son, of the father, and the lesson that the Master would teach. The son found that living the life of the senses, uncontrolled by the mind and the spirit, did not pay. He found that excesses did not pay, and in this he was thoroughly disillusioned. He found that violation of these laws carried its own penalty, and he paid dearly.

Dejection and suffering came, and his better self then had a chance to assert itself. He realized how much better he had been, and how much better off he would be, at his father's home — his own home, The resolve came and back he went.

The father might have said: 'Well, my son, . . . you've learned your lesson, haven't you? I'm glad you have. In the future . . .' He might have thought it, but he knew that the son knew it as well as he, and he probably felt that confidence, an active mental force, would be of greater help to the son than anything he could say. Love is his predominating characteristic. He never forgets his child and has looked often for his return.

The day comes when his love and his faith are rewarded. Instantly he recognizes that figure, though far down the road. 'My boy who was dead is alive again and is coming home!' Instead of waiting in a dignified way, his overwhelming love impels him down the road, and he runs to welcome him, and in the joy of his love the son senses his father's pardon.

And this is the truth that the Master would point in this incomparable parable: Forgiveness of sin is of the very nature of a living and loving God. No sacrifice to be made, no burnt offerings, no blood of a slain lamb, no ordeal in connection with an individual or organization, no tribute money — it is a spiritual matter between a man and his God. To see his folly, to repent, to turn from his errors and transgressions — genuinely to seek forgiveness, secures forgiveness.

There is another aspect of truth that the Master brings out when a man seeks divine forgiveness: forgiveness will be his, if he in turn has the heart and disposition to forgive; and in this way he drives home the necessity of an essential human quality.

A part of the brief and fundamental prayer that he taught is: 'And forgive us our debts, as we also have forgiven our debtors.' And following very close upon this he added: 'For if ye forgive men their trespasses, your heavenly Father will also forgive you: but if ye forgive not men their trespasses, neither will your heavenly Father forgive your trespasses. (Matt. 6:14-15)

Chapter 8

'I am a Man as You are'

Joyfully the Master trod the highways, with a deep-set faith and a burning zeal in the pursuit of his mission: the good news of the Kingdom which, if men would hear and recognize, would not only save them from their sins, but would lead them into a knowledge of the fuller, richer life that he would have them attain.

Sometimes it was to an individual he spoke, sometimes to a little group, sometimes to a great throng of persons who pressed hard in their eagerness one upon another. Always confident, knowing the source of the truth which he proclaimed, confident always of his power through a complete reliance upon the divine power within that he realized and that he taught, he nevertheless never allowed an inflated ego, that vice of fools, to manifest itself in him. He was always humble. Numbers of times and in various circumstances he took pains to make this plain.

'As he was going forth into the way, there ran one to him, and kneeled to him, and asked him, Good Master, what shall I do that I may inherit eternal life? And Jesus said unto him, Why callest thou me good? None is good save one, that is God.' (Mark 10: 7-28)

On another occasion while he was teaching a group that had gathered around him, one old fellow, it is related, got so enthusiastic, or so emotional, that he fell down and began to worship him.

Seeing him, that same sense of personal humility, combined perhaps with amusement, or pity, prompted the Master to say in substance: 'No, no, don't do that. Get up. Don't do that. I am a man as you are. And how clear-cut but how telling is his insight and his teaching along this same line!

'When thou art bidden of any man to a marriage feast, sit not down in the chief seat; lest haply a more honourable man than thou be bidden of him, and he that bade thee and him come and say to thee, Give this man place; and then thou begin with shame to take the lowest place. But when thou art bidden, go and sit down in the lowest place; that when he that hath bidden thee cometh, he may say to thee, Friend, go up higher; then shalt thou have glory in the presence of all that sit at meat with thee. For every one that exalteth himself shall be humbled; and he that humbleth himself shall be exalted. (Luke 14:8-11)

Again the personal simplicity of the Master is shown.

'Take my yoke upon you, and learn of me; for I am meek and lowly in heart.' (Matt, 11:29) Another interesting lesson in simplicity and humility and their significance, in a little different light, is pointed by him.

'Two men went up into the temple to pray; the one a Pharisee, and the other a publican. The Pharisee stood and prayed thus with himself, God, I thank thee, that I am not as other men are, extortionist, unjust, adulterers, or even as this publican. I fast twice in the week; I give tithes of all that I possess. And the publican, standing afar off, would not lift so much as his eyes unto heaven, but smote upon his breast, saying, God be merciful to me a sinner. I tell you, this man went down to his house justified rather than the other; for every one that exalteth himself shall be abased; and he that humbleth himself shall be exalted.' (Luke 18:10-14)

The verse immediately preceding the Master's words reads: 'And he spoke this parable unto certain which trusted in themselves that they were righteous, and despised others.'

And still again, along this same general line, how universally applicable and how simple and how clear-cut his statement:

'Judge not, that ye be not judged. For with what judgment ye judge, ye shall be judged: and with what measure ye mete, it shall be measured to you again. And why beholdeset thou the mote that is in thy brother's eye, but considerest not the beam that is in thine own eye? Or how wilt thou say to thy brother, Let me pull out the mote out of thine eye; and behold, a beam is in thine own eye. Thou hypocrite, first cast out the beam out of thine own eye; and then shalt thou see clearly to cast out the mote out of thy brother's eye.' (Matt. 7:1-5)

There was something supremely refreshing and simple in the mind of the Master as far as the personal self is concerned. When it came, though, to the great truth he had realized and felt he embodied and endeavoured so eagerly to reveal to others, we have something of a different tone — something to which he would have all men give attention. He then becomes the voice, the advocate. of God with his Gospel, his good news - 'my Father's business.'

Ascending from the personal. Jesus to the full realization of the Christ, he speaks with a sense of the power which that realization gives. He changes the expression that he so generally applied to himself, son of man, to the form, son of God. He makes clear, however, the basis of it: 'Of myself I can do nothing; it is the Father that worketh in me, my Father works and I work.'

The Christ consciousness — 'I and my Father are one' — now assumes complete mastery; and dedicating his life to the proposition as he states it, 'as I am you shall be,' and enlisting at once the attention of men, he sets forth his claims and his authority for them:

'To this end have I been born, and to this end am I come into the world, that I should bear witness unto the truth." (John 18:37)

'I came to cast fire upon the earth; and how I would that it were already kindled.' (Luke 12:49)

'I do nothing of myself, but as the Father taught me, I speak these things.' (John 8:28)

'My teaching is not mine, but his that sent me. If any man willeth to do his will, he shall know of the teaching, whether it be of God, or whether I speak from myself. He that speaketh from himself seeketh his own glory; but he that seeketh the glory of him that sent him, the same is true, and no unrighteousness is in him.' (John 7:16-18)

'I am the bread of life: he that cometh to me shall never hunger; and he that believeth on me shall never thirst.' (John 6:35)

'Come unto me, all ye that labour and are heavy laden, and I will give you rest. Take my yoke upon you, and learn of me; for I am meek and lowly in heart: and ye shall find rest unto your souls. For my yoke is easy, and my burden is light.' (Matt. 11:28-30)

'If ye abide in my word, then are ye truly my disciples; and ye shall know the truth, and the truth shall make you free.' (John 8:31-32)

'I am the resurrection, and the life: he that believeth in me, though he were dead, yet shall he live: and whosoever liveth and belicveth in me shall never die.' (John 9:25-26)

'He that heareth my word, and believeth hath passed out of death into life.' (John 5:24)

'The words that I speak unto you, they are spirit, and they are life. (John 6:63)

Every word, every parable, every teaching of the Way-shower had for its ultimate purpose the bringing of his message of God into the troubled lives of his hearers. He was the door through which they could enter. He was the light that would light their consciousness to this Kingdom within.

One day as he taught, there was a commotion and he stopped to listen, while a smile perhaps played over the faces of his audience. A certain woman of the company lifted up her voice and said unto him: 'Blessed is the womb that bore thee, and the paps which thou

hast sucked.' But he said: 'Yea rather, blessed are they that hear
the word of God, and keep it.' (Luke 11:27-28) A friendly inter-
change, perhaps, but a genuine earnestness on the part of both.

Practically everything centered around his great fundamental
message, his Gospel, his good news of the consciousness of God
in the minds, the hearts, the souls of men: the finding of this Kingdom within and the results that would follow.

He was not so much a teacher of morality as he was a prophet,
an adventurer in truth, who was bringing to the world a new truth,
so to speak, a truth so fundamental that when actually received
and acted upon it would touch, modify, and direct every act and
phase of life. It would bring a positive gain and security, while un-
belief resulting in its rejection would bring loss or even desolation.

So convinced is he of this fact that he boldly proclaims:

'Everyone that heareth these words of mine, and doeth them,
shall be likened unto a wise man, who built his house upon the
rock: and the rain descended, and the floods came, and the winds
blew, and beat upon that house; and it fell not: for it was founded
upon the rock. And everyone that heareth these words of mine,
and doeth them not, shall be likened unto a foolish man, who built
his house upon the sand: and the rain descended, and the floods
came, and the winds blew, and smote upon that house; and it fell:
and great was the fall thereof.' (Matt. 7:24-27)

'Work not for the meat which perisheth, but for the meat which
abideth unto eternal life, which the Son of man shall give unto
you.' (John 6:27)

And how simply and clearly he points out the gain in the better
and more abiding things of life!

'Lay not up for yourselves treasures upon the earth, where moth
and rust consume and where thieves break through and steal: but
lay up for yourselves treasures in heaven, where neither moth nor
rust doth consume, and where thieves do not break through and
steal: for where thy treasure is, there will thy heart be also. The
lamp of the body is the eye: if therefore thine eye be single, thy
whole body shall be full of light. But if thine eye be evil, thy whole
body shall be full of darkness. If therefore the light that is in thee
be darkness, how great is the darkness! No man can serve two
masters: for either he will hate the one, and love the other; or else
he will hold to one, and despise the other. Ye cannot serve God
and mammon.' (Matt. 6:19-24)

A certain steadfastness and moral fiber is required, he says.

'No man having put his hand to the plough, and looking back, is fit for the Kingdom of God. (Luke 9:62)

His injunction to any who would be his follower is to put first things first.

'He said unto a certain man, Follow me. But he said, Lord, suffer me first to go and bury my father. But he said unto him, Leave the dead to bury their own dead; but go thou and publish abroad the Kingdom of God.' (Luke 9:59-60)

Men must be not only receivers but must be doers of the word. They must not only enter into this new consciousness, this new birth, but they must let it have an unceasing grip on their lives. They must not only believe, but they must do. They must not only receive the truth, but they must live the life. If the truth take real hold of the life, it will push the life out into action, he affirms.

'Whosoever will come after me, let him deny himself, and take up his cross, and follow me. For whosoever will save his life shall lose it; but whosoever shall lose his life for my sake and the gospel's, the same shall save it. For what shall it profit a man if he shall gain the whole world, and lose his own soul? Or what shall a man give in exchange for his soul?' (Mark 8:34-37)

He had great confidence not only in the redeeming power but in the endurance of the truth that he brings.

'Heaven and earth shall pass away: but my words shall not pass away. (Mark 13:31)

He felt that the truth he had realized and was bringing to the world had a timeless element. He felt that this truth was so fundamental and was so practical in its elevating and helpful power in the individual life, and also in the collective life of the people, that he was willing even to give his life for it; and as events proved, when the final clash came with the entrenched organization of privilege and enervating dogma, he did die for it. There can be no greater evidence of his mastering belief as to how helpful and valuable the truth he brought might be in the lives of men and women everywhere.

It would not only be of help in the everyday problems and affairs of life, but it would redeem them from their misconceptions and sins and errors of life.

To repent and then to believe and to follow his truth meant forgiveness and the beginning of a new life. Their sins were thereby forgiven, and they should be forgotten; even the recollection of them with its benumbing, beclouding, and enervating influence was to cease and to give place to the joy that his living truth would bring. It was simply to turn and to follow the truth, which would become as a light to their heretofore stumbling feet.

To turn also from the blind leaders of the blind, the ecclesiastical peddlers of a lifeless system of form and inconsequential observances, and to follow this truth, this light of life that he brought, would make their redemption complete. There was no scheme of salvation; rather, he bitterly condemned those who would make a pretense of such — especially as the perquisites of any institution.

'Woe unto you, scribes and Pharisees . . . for ye shut the Kingdom of Heaven against men: for ye enter not in yourselves, neither suffer ye them that are entering in to enter.' (Matt. 23:13)

'Ye blind guides,' he said of those he had just described and warned against; 'ye blind guides, which strain at a gnat, and swallow a camel.'

That, a man's life, even in his wanderings away from the Father's fold, is a matter between him and his Father, and that his return brings joy not only to himself and all whom his life touches, but primarily to the Father, he sets forth simply and beautifully in his parable as related by Luke:

'What man of you, having an hundred sheep, if he lose one of them, doth not leave the ninety and nine in the wilderness, and go after that which is lost, until he find it? And when he hath found it, he layeth it on his shoulders, rejoicing. And when he cometh home, he calleth together his friends and neighbours, saying unto them, Rejoice with me; for I have found my sheep which was lost. I say unto you, that likewise joy shall be in heaven over one sinner that repenteth, more than over ninety and nine just persons, which need no repentance.' (Luke 15:4-7)

No less significant and interesting, as he states it, is the truth in the parable that immediately follows:

'Either what woman having ten pieces of silver, if she lose one piece, doth not light a candle, and sweep the house, and seek diligently till she find it? And when she hath found it, she calleth her friends and her neighbours together, saying, Rejoice with me; for I have found the piece which I had lost. Likewise, I say unto you, there is joy in the presence of the angels of God over one sinner that repenteth. (Luke 15:8-10)

A friend, a man of great interests, very observant and understanding, believes that the sole purpose of life is experience. It is one of his cardinal beliefs — quite as basic as is his belief in reincarnation, which in turn has to do with experience. Its real personal value lies, of course, in what one chooses to make of each experience.

The Master throws many a light for guidance here - in The Way.

Chapter 9
Sons of Men Living as Sons of God

It was the element of human service that fired the life of the Way-shower, and that continually led him on. He felt his leadership, his mastery, undoubtedly, and perhaps his greatness, but it was always subservient to his own dictum: He that is greatest among you shall be he who serves. Hence there was ever that splendid humility which is always found with real power and real greatness.

He made it plain that he had something that they did not possess, but that he was the same as they were. And when he said, 'I and my Father are one, again he said, 'as I am you shall be.'

Through a rare understanding, through an illumined and exalted vision of life, he took his real pedigree from God, but he always remembered he was a man. This is a vital part of both his message and his value, to us men of earth. This, when we understand him and his purpose aright, is what makes him no enigma. This is what makes him the Great Teacher, the Master, the revealer of the truth that the Divine life of God is the life that is man.

Every man is a potential son of God: to realize this, to be born from above, is the saving grace that changes the potentiality into the reality. Man is saved thereby from his lower conceptions and wanderings and blunders, and this Divine realization makes him heir to the guidance, the help, the power, the supply, that pertains to the universal Source. Hence: seek first the Kingdom of God and His righteousness, the Kingdom of God within, and all other things shall be added unto you.

This truth that I bring you, he said in effect, that the Kingdom of God is within you, makes clear, alive, and potent the truth that man is created in the image and likeness of God. But God is Spirit, as I have said, and spirit is life — the Universal Spirit and power of life that manifests itself, as individual spirit, in man. He taught what he had uniquely and so abundantly found: the conscious union with the Father's life as the one and all-inclusive thing.

The Kingdom of God and His righteousness, the Kingdom within, is not only what he came to teach, but what he clearly and unmistakably and in many varied forms did teach. 'He went about through cities and villages, preaching and bringing the good tidings of the Kingdom of God.' He had a great vision and faith in its value and power — 'And this gospel of the Kingdom shall be preached in the whole world, for a testimony unto all nations.'

It is on account of man's not knowing this inner fountain of life, this light of the Spirit, or on account of his departing from it, that sin and error and the sense of sin, that disease and fears and forebodings, that heart-pain and hunger creep in and assume the mastery. Things become hidden, uncertainties abound, perplexities prevail, because the mind and the spirit are not awake to the light that lighteth every man who cometh into the world, available for every man who desires, seeks, and follows the light.

'I am that light,' he said, 'through the knowledge of this gospel of the Kingdom that I bear witness to.' This he said of himself, as the giver of the light-bearing truth which he so clearly taught. The light that will radiate from this inner Centre will make you always sure of your way.

'I am the light of the world; he that followeth me shall not walk in darkness, but shall have the light of life.' (John 8:12) He longs for men to get his central truth, and he tries so hard to make it plain, and what it will do for them.

It was an earlier prophet who said: 'The spirit of man is the candle of the Lord.' The son of man through the light that had been given to him, and that made him uniquely the son of God, would light this candle in all other men, so that they too might become sons of God, born from above, becoming in turn a light for other men.

This he expected of those who would be his real followers, for he said: 'Let your light so shine before men, that they seeing your good work may glorify your Father in heaven.' It was a great truth, redemptive, building, saving, and he would give his life if need be to establish it in men's minds. No man perhaps has ever had a greater sense of human service.

No man perhaps has been so supremely an exemplar for other men. From first to last, from early to late — 'Know you not that I must be about my Father's business?' It is wonderful — my Father and your Father. Call no man your father upon the earth, for one is your Father, even God. It is wonderful. You are heir of the Eternal. Your Kingdom awaits you. You are a creature of sin and a worm of the dust only if you think you are. I bring you knowledge of your Divine sonship.

The time was ripe in the evolution of the race for another step up to be made, the step in consciousness from the natural man to the spiritual man. In Christ Jesus was that peculiar combination through which this could be effected. His unusual intuitive perception united to a clear-seeing mind — this combined with an humbleness of spirit and a deep sense of comradeship resulted in making him an evangel, a teacher, so great that he becomes the Way- shower and, in truth, the saviour of all to whose minds and hearts his revelation makes an appeal.

This new and larger perception of life so filled and so thrilled him that with a mighty urge it pushed him out into the highways and byways of his native Galilee, and to Judea to the south where the Temple of his people was, proclaiming as he went, 'I am come that you might have life and that you might have it more abundantly.'

This he did with an earnestness, a persuasiveness that thrilled men's souls for well-nigh three years. And the common people heard him gladly — sometimes too gladly, or so it would seem — and in such numbers that he inevitably ran up against the entrenched ecclesiastical system of the priests of the temple. They, realizing that it meant interference with their authority and their living, killed him. He cared more for the truth and its saving value to his people, and eventually through them to the world, than he did for his own life.

'I must be about my Father's business,' My Father's business is to make Him known to you, my brothers — my Father and your Father. You are ignorant of who and what you are. The Infinite spirit of life, the life of God the Father, is the life that is in you. That is my realization; this is my revelation to you.

If you will believe my word, if you will receive this my truth, if you will live in this realization, you will not only receive me and be my disciples, but you will be born anew, born from above, and you will enter into the power and the glory of the Kingdom of God and His righteousness — and righteousness means right living. And then, as I have said, all other things, good things, needed things, true things, shall be added unto you.

It is the Kingdom of Heaven — and heaven means harmony. You are living in harmony with the Father's life — son of man living, joyously living, as son of God. It is simple. There is nothing complex. Believe me. My teaching is not mine, but His that sent me. I am come in my Father's name.

'Whosoever drinketh of the water that I shall give him shall never thirst; but the water that I shall give him shall become in him a well of water springing up unto eternal life.'

A wonderful statement, a wonderful promise; but it is given by one who drank deep at the Source, and it is given with splendid assurance.

Every man must stand in some relation to his Maker. We men and women of today should, almost beyond calculation, be grateful that we have one of the character and the stature of Jesus of Galilee as our helper and guide. A life beyond reproach, un-self-centered, uniquely equipped for finding and knowing God in his own life, so filled with love for his fellow men, that the great purpose and passion of his life became to make known to others this greatest and most valuable thing that can be known.

The certainty of this knowledge and its tremendous help in his own life should make his words come with such convincing authority as to lift a great burden of uncertainty and responsibility from our own minds and lives. And the beauty of it is that each of us, if we be genuinely interested and in earnest, may quickly test the truth and the value — the concrete, everyday-life value — of his revelation.

Moreover, we may rest assured that one of his splendid mind and insight and spirit would not — and entirely of his own accord — spend his life in imparting this to others, if he did not thoroughly realize and understand its value — not only its truth, but its value.

Yes, we may rest in the assurance that the Master knew whereof he spoke, and that his promises are true. He realized and he knew the life of God first-hand. With him there was never any harking back to someone else, to some past age of formulation; never even 'The prophets have said.'

It was his experience of God first-hand that makes him speak with authority, the authority that grips our interest, our confidence, and our faith in him, and our allegiance to his great human-divine message.

It is no small privilege for uncertain, confused, and mystified men to be enabled to know God, and the life and the power and the joy of His Kingdom, from such a source — the supreme Way-shower for all who would know 'The Way.'

Chapter 10
A Source of his Genius

Joshua Ben Joseph, he of the little carpenter's shop of his father Joseph at Nazareth, has travelled far, though not wide, during the well-nigh three years of his teaching ministry. An almost irresistible impulse, impelled always by love, has taken him up and down dusty and often hot roads of Judea and Peraea and his own Galilee. It is but a small area; an area all told about a hundred and fifty miles long and a hundred miles wide. He early felt the impulse to leave his native village of Nazareth, and made Capernaum, some few miles distant, the central point of his goings and his comings.

During this time he was going almost continually here and there, the sower of the seed of what he felt was a mighty truth in the minds of all types and conditions of men and women and many times it was a motley crowd that gathered to hear him. He eagerly hoped, but sometimes almost in despair, that the truth he sought to plant would, when he would no longer be here to plant it, be taken by other men in order that it might reach a still larger hearing.

His experiences were many and varied; always interesting, sometimes amusing, sometimes discouraging — many times discouraging had he been one of a lesser mould. Had he been one of lesser vision and lesser faith, the memory of his experience twice repeated in his native place, and among his own home people, would have cost him considerable discomfort or even sadness.

The ties of human friendship do count. To be misunderstood and turned against by the people where one has been born, where one has worked and has grown to manhood, is unpleasant and discouraging. To be misunderstood, to be questioned and to that extent unappreciated by one's own mother and brothers and sisters, is not agreeable to experience or later to remember.

One account of the carpenter's son returned to his native village is given by the writer Luke, and it is interesting to read it in the form it is given: 'And he came to Nazareth, where he had been brought up: and, as his custom was, he went into the synagogue on the Sabbath day, and stood up for to read. And there was delivered unto him the book of the prophet Esaias. And when he had opened the book, he found the place where it was written, The Spirit of the Lord is upon me, because he hath anointed me to preach the Gospel to the poor; he hath sent me to heal the broken-hearted, to preach deliverance to the captives, and recovering of sight to the blind, to set at liberty them that are bruised, to preach the acceptable year of the Lord. And he closed the book, and he gave it again to the minister, and sat down. And the eyes of all them that were in the synagogue were fastened on him. And he began to say unto them, This day is this Scripture fulfilled in your ears. And all bare him witness, and wondered at the gracious words which proceeded out of his mouth. And they said, Is not this Joseph's son?

'And he said unto them, Ye will surely say unto me this proverb, physician, heal thyself: whatsoever we have heard done in Capernaum, do also here in thy country. And he said, Verily I say unto you, No prophet is accepted in his own country. But I tell you of a truth, many widows were in Israel in the days of Elias, when the heaven was shut up three years and six months, when great famine was throughout all the land; but unto none of them was Elias sent, save unto Sarepta, a city of Sidon, unto a woman that was a widow. And many lepers were in Israel in the time of Eliseus the prophet; and none of them was cleansed, saving Naaman the Syrian.

'And all they in the synagogue, when they heard these things, were filled with wrath, and rose up, and thrust him out of the city, and led him unto the brow of the hill whereon their city was built, that they might cast him down head long. But he passing through the midst of them went his way, and came down to Capernaum, a city of Galilee, and taught them on the Sabbath days. And they were astonished at his doctrine: for his word was with power.' (Luke 4:16-32)

This account is interesting not only from its pathos but from the standpoint of giving us a very clear-cut picture of exactly how Jesus was regarded, while he lived, by the people with whom he lived.

To follow tradition is at times to traduce the fact or the person that we are not able, through intellectual indifference or intellectual cowardice, rightly to apprise or understand. It but encourages the reign of even the manufacture of dogma, that deadly thing which the Master himself found was throttling the spirit, the life and the welfare of his people, and the vigorous denunciation of which eventually cost him his life.

Nineteen hundred years is a very short period in the great march of time, and God's eternal laws, laws of the universe, laws of human life, laws of human generation, were the same then as they are now. We can rest assured that what does not occur now did not occur then. To be born of a virgin, with God, or some god, or some mythological character, as father, was a very common occurrence in the traditions of antiquity.

Buddha, six hundred years before Jesus' time, was born of a virgin. So tradition said later, after he became thoroughly well-known and needed to be explained. So tradition said, when the priest began to mould a revelation and teaching, of wonderful light and power for human help, into a dogmatic system shot through with a material tinge — with an eye to authority, power, and money. Buddhism suffered great degeneration from the high ideals and humanly helpful purposes of him upon whose name it was built.

Practically all the world's great leaders and saviours later were followed by this same tradition. Considerably before the time of Jesus and continuing many years afterward, to be born of a virgin was the fame of numbers of rulers and emperors. Very few were immune. Caesar Augustus was reputed the son of God born of a virgin mother. Such was the very common belief of the time, because tradition said it.

Jesus knew himself, and all of his time knew him, as the son of Joseph and Mary. Mary herself states it on several occasions, or at least from her statements we can infer nothing else

— and she probably knew — yes, she undoubtedly knew. She was no simpleton. Jesus went with Mary and Joseph as a boy to Jerusalem, and lingered in the temple while they started home supposing him to be in the company. When they missed him and going back found him, the account reads: 'And his mother said unto him, Son, why hast thou thus dealt with us? Behold thy father and I have sought thee sorrowing.' (Luke 2:48) As a boy and while he lived at Nazareth, he was known as Joshua Ben Joseph.

The parents, the family, were poor, but from the most trustworthy accounts that we have, they were well known and well regarded. The parents were perhaps at times hard pressed; to care for a family of nine from the proceeds of a little carpenter's shop in a village of that size was no small problem; and the help of Joshua, the oldest of the children, before any of the others were sufficiently grown to contribute to the family's support, must have been a godsend.

That he received a splendid inheritance of qualities from such

parents there can be no doubt — a splendid combination of qualities of spirit, of mind, and of body which gave him that unique
endowment of power for discerning the things of the mind and the
spirit, a mind for clear-cut seeing and statement, and a vigorous, healthy body through which all could function to their
highest.

His must have been a unique endowment among the sons of
men, an endowment which he in turn appreciated and used to its
highest, which enabled him so uniquely to become a son of God,
and so splendidly and triumphantly a revealer of the truth of God;
or rather, shall we say, an embodiment and revealer of the truth
of God.

We can well imagine that the clear-seeing vigour of his mind
would make him the foe of anything that would separate him from
his fellows and so lessen his power of appeal. The only point of
difference he would countenance would be that a great truth had
been given to him, a truth which so illumined and enlarged and
filled his life that he was its wayshower so that it might give freedom and the same larger life to those who would hear him. When
he saw the need of his people, and the low level of life around him
compared to this larger life which had been revealed to him, it was
but natural and right that he should come to feel himself the Messiah, the anointed, the son of God, for the deliverance of his people
from their mental and spiritual bondage.

And when through the truth that he taught and the works that
he did, his fame spread far and wide, and he began to be looked
upon as the leader, the deliverer, the Messiah for whom they had
long and intently been waiting, he went out of his way to make it
plain, time and time again, that his message was a spiritual message, that the Kingdom of God he was showing them was a spiritual and not a material kingdom.

He never succumbed, and never had the slightest inclination
to succumb, to the dream of grandeur which before and since af-
flicted so many able but lesser minds. 'My Kingdom is not of this
world,' he said many times. Always he felt himself the servant of
the truth which had been given to him, and felt that he must offer
it every ounce of his devotion. He did this with such a steadfast
purpose that nothing savouring of a material kingdom ever had
the slightest lure for him or influence upon him. Here again appears the real genius and the real caliber of the man.

This we do know, however — and it is the fact of real importance
and value: he had a great genius, a great aptitude in the realm of

the mind and the spirit in knowing life, which he identified with God, or 'the Father.' He had an unusual perception of reality. He perceived being as spirit, and spirit as the universal creative force or energy which manifests itself as life, life energizing and disclosing itself in all individual forms. This he perceived was the life that was his.

God is Spirit, he said, and spirit is life. In a perfectly natural way, then, he identified his life with the life of God — not through any reasoning process but through the direct process of self-consciousness, of intuition. He was not only a genius, but a great genius, in this realm .

A genius is one who finds his goal not through precepts or pattern or example, but through the direct method of inner-seeing, of intuition. That inner perceptive quality of the mystic is his prompter and his guide.

Some years ago a most interesting life of the Master, or study of his life, was written by a friend of mine, a woman of unusual perceptive qualities, one thoroughly unbiased and devoted to truth. After a long period of preparation, she found in him the high order of the mystic. Her thought is of particular interest and value at this point:

'Even in his own age Jesus was recognized as a mystic — one to whom knowledge comes not by way of reason and objective sense, but by a faculty of in-knowing. . . . He easily knew and did what other men fumble and strive for. He had a genius for mystically acquired knowledge of God in His relation to man. He is without doubt the greatest mystical genius that ever lived. . . Jesus saw God as no man before him. He saw God as the Father and man as the veritable son; God-stuff in man, He in us and we in Him. . . . Jesus was an Occidental mystic whose mysticism is toward the mastery of life rather than the evasion of it. . . . On the whole, his concept of the experienceable universe has had a larger share of acceptance, and maintains itself in the thought stream longer, than the concepts of the intelligible universe predicated by Plate and Aristotle. The cornerstone of his mystical knowing, the oneness of the nature of God, conceived as Spirit, and man the projection of that Spirit into the world of sense, has become the head of the foundation of modern science; spirit and matter, energy and form, one substance, not denied by Jew nor infidel nor any other persuasion.'

Again consider this thought of hers - still more valuable perhaps because of its individual and practical element:

'Knowing God as spirit, and love as the mode of his being, and man a partaker of God's nature, Jesus also believed man to be a partaker of God's powers. It is impossible to set aside the evidence that, in relation to the exigencies of his destiny as well as his daily life, Jesus lived at a high level of personal efficiency, and that he undertook to teach his disciples how to attain and sustain such levels for themselves. More than any man before or since, Jesus came teaching that the mystical is the practical. All those high moods which had been the prerogatives of saints and prophets, he meant to make part of the common use and posesssion. Mind, Spirit, whatever it is constituting the fundamental alikeness of God and man, he established as the daily instrument, accessible alike to the learned and the unlearned. God is as free as air, and heaven as close at hand in a fishing smack as in Jerusalem. . . . He drew — though his name people have not accepted it — all the manifestations of the supernatural into the field of the natural. But Jesus did nothing which he did not openly declare to be commonly possible, the fulfilling of a natural law. As far as he proved God, he declared Him, and he knew and said that there might be those of his disciples who by the same means might do greater wonders. . . .

'It was the mystical life that Jesus admonished his disciples to lead, as differentiated from the ritualistic, legalistic life of the devout Jew. "Know yourselves and ye shall be aware that ye are the sons of the Father. . . ." They were to abide in this consciousness of God within, and it was to be sufficient unto them in health and fortune, food and raiment. There was no limitation to the power of God in man, and therefore no concept of limitation was to be allowed to the sincere disciple.

'In all or any of the exigencies of human life you were to ask and you would receive. Knock and it should be opened unto you. Jesus made no distinction whatever as to the nature of these exigencies, whether they were of hunger, or disease, or what are called moral problems.'

Chapter 11
Rich Toward God

Joshua Ben Joseph, the prophet of Galilee, never forgets that he is from and of the people. After the rather distressing incident which occurred when in his ministry he went back to his native village of Nazareth, and gave or tried to give in the little village synagogue the same message he had been giving in many parts of Galilee, and in Judaea to the south, he seems to have broken with his home people and with his family. In a common-sense manner he recognized the inhospitality of their thought and the feeling at times even of hostility. Anyway he seems not to have gone back.

Once when he was near again an incident occurred which throws additional light upon these facts. At one house where a large gathering had assembled, the press of the people was so great that he and the disciples who were with him could scarcely eat. The account as given by Mark is: 'And the multitude cometh together again, so that they could not so much as eat bread. And when his friends heard of it, they went out to lay hold on him: for they said, He is beside himself.'

So independent, so unconventional, so unorthodox was he, both in his teaching and in his practices, that many times a great commotion was stirred, and at times there was a considerable wagging of tongues. He mingled with publicans and sinners; be even ate with them. This disgusted the well-to-do, those of social standing, and particularly the scribes and Pharisees. And his teachings to the congregations assembled in the synagogues, humble and so different from the conventional type, gave rise to many questions and discussions, offending some and especially these same scribes and Pharisees. Many a time the question arose: 'What manner of man is this?'

These same things were felt undoubtedly by the members of his own family, his mother and his brothers, humble people that they were. They were disturbed by the rumours which were brought to them. They could not understand. They did not like the wagging of the village tongues. They would have him come home rather than risk the disgrace that might come to them. They were incapable evidently of understanding his larger mission, and the passion that filled his soul to carry on with it. He was aware of this feeling. He perhaps regretted it, but he could not help it. He perhaps foresaw that some time he might be compelled even to break with them. His convictions and the absorbing purpose of his life, even if they could not understand, gave him his direction.

At the meeting in the same house, there was a clash with some of the scribes and Pharisees, who, hearing of the work that he was doing and the great crowds that were following him, had come or had been sent up from Jerusalem. Later, while he was teaching there was an interruption. The account is given by Mark: 'There came then his brethren and his mother, and, standing without, sent unto him, calling him. And the multitude sat about him, and they say unto him, 'Behold, thy mother and thy brethren without seek for thee.' And he answered them, saying, 'Who is my mother and my brethren? . . . For whosoever shall do the will of God, the same is my brother, my sister, and mother.' (Mark 3:31-35)

One grasps here the clear understanding which prompted his statement after his chilly reception the last time he visited his home town — and how pointed and how definite he makes it: 'A prophet is not without honour, but in his own country, and among his own kin, and in his own house.' (Mark 6:4)

He understood — but something bigger pushed him on: human needs. 'When Jesus saw the multitudes, he was moved with compassion on them, because they were distressed and scattered, as sheep not having a shepherd.' Human needs — and those the most in need.

'It came to pass, that he was sitting at meat in Levi's house, and many publicans and sinners sat down with Jesus and his disciples: for there were many, and they followed him. And the scribes and the Pharisees, when they saw that he was eating with the sinners and publicans, said unto his disciples, He eateth and drinketh with publicans and sinners, And when Jesus heard it, he saith unto them, They that are whole have no need of a physician, but they that are sick: I came not to call the righteous, but sinners to repentance.' (Mark 2:15-17)

He knew their needs. He would make them rich toward God. And then the other extreme, for each has its needs.

'Take heed, and keep yourselves from all covetousness: for a man's life consisteth not in the abundance of the things which he possesseth. And he spoke a parable unto them, saying, The ground of a certain rich man brought forth plentifully: and he reasoned within himself, saying, What shall I do, because I have not where to bestow my fruits? And he said, This will I do: I will pull down my barns, and build greater; and there will I bestow all my corn and my goods. And I will say to my soul, Soul, thou hast much goods laid up for many years; take thine ease, eat, drink, be merry. But God said unto him, Thou foolish one, this night thy soul shall be required of thee; and the things which thou hast prepared, whose shall they be? So is he that layeth up treasure for himself, and is not rich toward God.' (Luke 12:15-21)

Rich toward God he would make him — for the present and for the future. Simple but mighty message. There was a universal quality in the message and in the personality of the Master that drew him to, and that drew to him, those of all conditions who needed help, rich or poor, humble or seemingly great. Occurrences even as he passed along the highway are interesting to observe.

'And Jesus entered and passed through Jericho. And, behold, there was a man called by name Zacchaeus; and he was a chief publican, and he was rich. And he sought to see Jesus who he was; and could not for the crowd, because he was little of stature. And he ran on before, and climbed up into a sycamore tree to see him: for he was to pass that way. And when Jesus came to the place, he looked up, and said unto him, Zacchaeus, make haste, and come down; for today I must abide at thy house. And he made haste, and came down, and received him joyfully. And when they saw it, they all murmured, saying, He is gone in to lodge with a man that is a sinner. And Zacchaeus stood, and said unto the Lord, Behold, Lord, the half of my goods I give to the poor; and if I have wrongfully exacted aught of any man, I restore fourfold, And Jesus said unto him, Today is salvation come to this house. (Luke 19:1-9)

Rich toward God, and still richer in that voluntarily he chose to do what was right! A beautiful understanding and comradeship between two sympathetic men! A name made immortal by the desire and the determination of an otherwise obscure man to know the best, and let it dominate his life!

Chapter 12
That Wonderful Friendship with the Twelve

Preceding the last phase of the Master's life here on earth a considerable change has taken place. His popularity is not so great as it was the preceding two or more years. He has many devoted followers, but the great crowds have fallen away. The frailty of human nature has played its part.

At one time the crowd had been so great, and the enthusiasm so unbounded, that then and there they would take him and make him King. Many a lesser man would have accepted it, would have justified himself and reached out to receive the scepter — entranced for the moment, and not foreseeing the trouble to main-tarn the kingship later on. Many a lesser mind would have succumbed to the 'dream of grandeur' and been willing to give battle to steal it, if need be, from another. Again the real genius of the Master asserts itself. His life and his truth have always to do, not with a material, but with a spiritual Kingdom. This is one reason why many of his former enthusiastic followers have fallen away from him.

Some begin to doubt, and justly, they think. If he is our deliverer, the Messiah, what has he done? What is he doing? For well-nigh three years now we have been following him and nothing has occurred. I am getting nothing out of it. Is he a false leader like others we have put our trust in — the others who have failed us? No well-to-do people, no respectable or rather leading people, with an exception here and there, are following him. The temple authorities do not endorse him. They do not even believe in him. They think and they openly say that he is an impostor. They are sending spies to watch him in order to get evidence that they may excommunicate him; for he is misleading the people, by teaching them things not in their formulated code. He even abuses them, calling them hypocrites, vipers, and children of vipers. Perhaps he has his reasons; but it bodes no good for us.

They say that the scribes and the Pharisees and the priests he speaks so bravely of — for good or ill God only knows — and even the high priest would kill him if they could find a charge sufficient to win the approval of the Roman authorities. They have cautioned him, they have dared him, they have warned him; but instead of being sensible he is growing bolder all the time. They say he is even thinking of going up to Jerusalem to do his teaching and his acts of healing right in their own sacred precincts. Little does he dream of their power. He either does not know or he does not think of the other teachers and prophets who have been killed, and quickly killed, for smaller offences.

Even his disciples, at least some of the twelve, begin to question and at times to weaken. Their patience is not inexhaustible, any more than their understanding at times of his teachings and his purpose. Where are they getting? What are they getting? They had left all to follow him. He has heard this repeated more than once. Misunderstandings between them, even rivalries, begin to take form. It requires at times the utmost patience on the part of the Master to cope with their unlettered ignorance.

Silently and patiently he bears with them, hoping always for the best and never losing his faith, but secretly wondering many times whether, when he is gone, they will be grown to sufficient stature to carry on. As he realizes that his time is growing shorter here, the more materially ambitious some of them seem to become. This costs him at times no little concern. Always patient and kind and trusting, he finds occasions when it seems necessary to administer an open rebuke. His understanding of human nature is so great, however, that he always bears with them. His supreme faith enables him always to trust them.

Even near the closing week two of the twelve, James and John, sons of thunder, come to him — and one account says the mother came with them — and say: 'Teacher, we would that thou shouldst do for us whatsoever we shall ask of thee.' And he said unto them, 'What would ye that I should do for you?' And they said unto him, 'Grant unto us that we may sit, one on thy right hand, and one on thy left hand, in thy glory.' Looking out for their own position, you see, and personal gain. Again it requires patience, patience and ingenuity, on the part of the Master.

The account continues: 'And when the ten heard it, they were moved with indignation against the two brethren.' Luke then later says that this same contention, amounting almost to a quarrel, continued even as they were gathered together at the last supper. On this same night, almost in astonishment, but gently as always, Jesus turned to Philip and said: 'Have I been so long a time with you and yet hast thou not known me?' Once to Peter he said: 'Are ye also without understanding?' Other related occurrences indicate all too clearly what he had to contend with. Then, at or near the end, one betrayed him, one denied him, and all the rest weakened and ran away, at least for the time being.

He had no thought of establishing an organization, a church — only a new knowledge and a new spirit that would bring a new life and a new vitality into the organization already established — yet he realized how much depended upon the group of twelve he had selected and had so patiently instructed in order that his truth might carry on. It is easy therefore to understand his great patience and his almost infinite faith in them; and it is a worthy and a fully deserved tribute to say that, later when the real test came, they did prove their first faith, and in a wonderful manner.

One of the most beautiful things in all history, with its touches of pathos, is the concern of the Master for the friendship and comradeship of this little band of rugged, untutored but earnest and receptive men as they ate together for the last time the feast of the Passover.

Superb and touching is his gratitude for their companionship and their confidence, his concern for their welfare and their safety, his faith that they would measure up to his expectations in using the truth that he would leave with them and, through them, with the world that he loved, and that in a few hours he knew he was to leave. And then his concern for them at the final brief parting scene at Gethsemane, near the gate, ready. When the officers of the Sanhedrin with the light of their torches come with his betrayer to arrest him, he says: 'I am he.' And he adds, for the disciples: 'If therefore ye seek me, let these go their way.'

We miss much of this close relationship if we do not get the full significance of his opening statement, when a few hours before he sat down with them in the upper room at the little inn where they were known and where they had often stayed before — to eat with them the last time: 'With desire I have desired to eat this Passover with you before I suffer.' (Luke 22:15) It was there that he gave them his final instructions, his final unfolding of the truth as it pertained to him and to them, the truth which knit them together in a bond of union that he felt would have in it a timeless element.

It was there that he threw into the Passover feast a personal element which would, he conceived, make an abiding and compelling memory of their life and work and fellowship together, for many years to come. He longs for this union, this comradeship, to live on, and above all for it to bind them to a carrying-on of the work, the spreading of his truth which they had laboured with him to accomplish.

He spoke as always in his own and their own Aramaic tongue. 'Eat my body and drink my blood,' in the Aramaic idiom, means, literally, endure suffering and hard work. It is a familiar form of expression still used by a small branch of the Assyrian people, who represent the oldest existing Christian Church; who think and talk in their native Aramaic tongue, and who today live almost identically the same life as did the people among whom Jesus was born and lived, and to whom he gave his message.

'I through my truth, my new message of life, am the new covenant' — this he would establish in their consciousness. Unquestionably we get the real and full purpose of the Master when we combine the true content of the Aramaic idiom with his injunction to his disciples, as they ate together this annual historic meal of their people. It was to be a binding together of their work, of their friendship, their comradeship, when they assembled together in another year to celebrate this same Passover feast. They were to do it remembering him, and to think of this, their last observance of it together.

Whether he intended it to be an observance for any others than his immediate group of disciples, no one but he will ever know — no one but he. That it has been frightfully abused in the past, the historic past, we all know. That today dogma has put into it a material content such as the spiritual sense of the Master never could have meant, and indeed would most bitterly condemn, we all know.

As a memorial of his life and his love, of the new covenant of his truth, impregnated always with the spiritual content which he intended, it can be made a very beautiful and sacred and useful sacrament. The fullness of its Aramaic meaning, the meaning which he had in mind to live in and to work for his truth — brings with it a saving power; saving for the life of the individual and saving for the life of the world. 'I am the light of the world,' he said, but he could be that only as each individual and a sufficient number of individuals should receive the truth and give it real being and expression in life.

In this and in all that went before, the essential genius of the Master and his one continuing purpose had to do with the things of the spirit. His great concern was that his teachings be so understood. He had to use material terms and illustrations, in order to get his meaning and his truth into the material, unspiritual minds of his hearers. And then many times he had to go back and explain to them the real spiritual import. Even his disciples were prone to drag his teachings down and interpret them in a material sense. He had to use terms with which they were familiar, terms and objects and forms of expression they knew, even at the risk of making his message liable at times to a material interpretation.

Chapter 13
Entry to Jerusalem - To Die

There was never any laziness in the young Rabbi prophet of Galilee. Prodigious was his zeal to carry his gospel, his good news, to needy people everywhere; and in a supreme manner he sensed the people's needs. From village to village, wherever he could be of greatest help, he went, The accounts indicate that the crowds seeking his help were sometimes very great:

'When Jesus saw the multitudes he was moved with compassion for them, because they were distressed and scattered, as sheep not having a shepherd. Then said he unto his disciples, 'the harvest truly is plenteous, but the labourers are few.' (Matt. 9:36-37)

His work must often have been very exhausting. Self-giving contact with people, especially in crowds, takes a great deal out of a sensitively organized person. A man of the open, Jesus sought quiet and rest and recuperation in the open; and outdoors he experienced those refreshing periods of prayer and communion by which he kept intact his sense of union with the Father. Time after time the accounts relate these occurrences:

'In the morning, a great while before day, he rose up and went out, and departed into a desert place, and there prayed. And Simon and they that were with him followed after him; and they found him, and say unto him, All are seeking thee. And he saith unto them, 'Let us go elsewhere into the next towns, that I may preach there also; for to this end came I forth.' (Mark 1:35-38)

When he had finished in one village, down the road he went to another, sometimes alone, sometimes with one or two, sometimes with more of his disciples. Eager he was always to fulfill his promise: 'Ye shall know the truth and the truth shall make you free — the truth of the life, the Kingdom of God, within; the truth not only to be accepted and believed, but also to be lived:

'By their fruits ye shall know them. Not everyone that saith unto me, Lord, Lord, shall enter into the Kingdom of Heaven; but he that doeth the will of my Father.' (Matt. 7:20-21)

Not only was he ever ready to share his truth with the people, but he was ever eager to free them and save them from the enervating and deadly dogma which was ceaselessly put about by the

priests and scribes and Pharisees. The world has perhaps never
seen a greater enemy of dogma than this herald of truth. He knew
that truth, his truth, and dogma could never exist together; and
he never hesitated to denounce its upholders and purveyors.

He knew how self-seeking and deadly they were both as individuals and as representatives of institutions. He knew how they lived
as parasites upon the people. 'Except your righteousness shall
exceed the righteousness of the scribes and Pharisees, ye shall in
no wise enter into the Kingdom of Heaven.' (Matt. 5:20) Inevitably
he aroused the enmity of those he so frequently denounced — at
times to their very faces. He was interfering with their authority, their business, their living.

More than once they had sent spies even from Jerusalem to
watch him, to catch him in a snare. They never succeeded, however, in doing this. So good a reader was he of human nature and
human motives, so clear in his in-seeing, that instead he
almost always confounded them. He had a growing sense of their
determination, as we say, to 'get' him. It did not appear to bother
him, and gradually he seemed to arrive at a point where he actually without fear courted an open conflict with them.

'From that time forth began Jesus to show unto his disciples,
how that he must go unto Jerusalem and suffer many things of the
elders and chief priests and scribes, and be killed.' (Matt. 16:21)

This was no idle statement on his part as it turned out. His
face was set toward Jerusalem and his disciples were to go with
him. The coming conflict might certainly mean his death, and he
planned it for a time when it might most reasonably occur.
The great annual festival ceremony of the Jews, the Passover,
was soon to be celebrated. He knew it was at Jerusalem that he
would be killed, and that there would be no better time or occasion. He alone knew that he was actually courting death.

His friends and followers in various localities warned him that
the temple authorities were seeking him, and advised him not to
go that year. Already the chief priests and the Pharisees, hearing how boldly he had denounced them, how he was teaching the
people not in their established religious code, and at times quite
contrary to it, and how great was the number of people now following him, had called a council at which Caiaphas, the chief priest,
spoke: 'If we let him alone,' he said, 'all men will believe on him:
and the Romans shall come and take away our place and nation.'
. . . .'Then from that day forth they took counsel together for to
put him to death. . . .And they watched him and sent forth spies,

which should feign themselves just men, that they might take hold of his words, that so they might deliver him unto the power and authority of the governor.'

This became quite generally known. There was also considerable talk and speculation throughout the countryside in many directions, just as there was at Jerusalem. Of one group which had already gone up in preparation for the feast the account reads: 'Then sought they for Jesus, and spoke among themselves, as they stood in the temple, What think ye, that he will not come to the feast?'

Six days then before the Passover we find Jesus and his disciples at Bethany, the home of his friends Mary and Martha and their brother Lazarus. Bethany is just outside Jerusalem whither they are bound, but a short walk away. Jesus knows then that at any time he is likely to be captured, to be tried, and to be put to death. He evidently has his own thoughts and plans about it, too; in fact he will see to it that he is arrested. He will do such things that the authorities cannot ignore him, even if they would.

They would probably find an easy ally to sanction their decree in the ruling Roman governor of Judea, Pontius Pilate, who not only detested Jews, but took pleasure in acts of violence and sometimes in executions without form of trial. It was Pilate who made his legions enter Jerusalem with figures of the God-Emperor emblazoned on their standards, notwithstanding his knowledge of how the Jews abhorred idolatry and graven images of any type.

But Tiberius Caesar, the God-Emperor, 'born of a virgin,' must have homage above every living man. It is interesting to note that the fiction of Tiberius being born of a virgin was known to Jesus and his followers and to the people of Jerusalem and Judaea, but that Jesus and his followers and all of the people knew nothing of the truth that he, Jesus, was born of a virgin. This was due to the fact that the knowledge connected with Jesus did not take form until a system of belief concerning him began to take definite form a number of years later.

It is the spring of the year in Judea, the month of Adar, and the festival spirit is in the air everywhere. All Jewry is on its way to the Holy City — in pilgrimage to celebrate the feast which takes their minds back to their people's escape from Egypt so many years ago.

From every hamlet and village and city, devoted bands are on their way, the great bulk are a- foot, the rich in litters, the bankers and merchants on camels. From the outermost parts of the then known earth, they come. From nearer by comes Herod; and Pontius Pilate from his official seat at Caesarea-by-the-sea; and minor and new Roman officials, eager to see this strange festival.

There are caravans fetching all kinds of goods for market with the hosts that will be in Jerusalem. Great loads of palm branches are brought from the growths along the Jordan, for decorations and the building of booths. The lanes and at places the highways are almost choked with lambs to be sold for the Pascal rite, heifers for sacrifice, and vendors of doves with their great towering crates. Music is in the air. A million and a half of pilgrims will eventually be in Jerusalem.

On the road leading down into the city from Olivet, Jesus comes with his disciples, heading a considerable band of his Galilean followers, among whom are a number of devoted women.

An interesting if not a strange thing now happens. Jesus sends back to the little village which they have just passed and where they have seen a colt standing, tied for hire as was common at this festival time, with instructions that it be brought to them. One account says an ass, one a donkey, one a colt — anyway, there is sufficient agreement to show that it was a four-footed creature and one that might be ridden.

Why did he do this? Did something come to his mind there that he had read in the scroll of the law and prophets, the scripture of the time, and did he half-venture himself as a fulfillment of prophecy? Or did he think it might please his followers? Or did he see that it would help him to achieve his end, his set purpose, of causing an annoying occurrence of which the authorities would hear, which they would perhaps witness, and of which in any event they would have to take cognizance? We do not know. It would not seem in the genius of the Master to do it for show.

At any rate, some of his followers threw clothes on the colt and sat him on it. The little procession then moved forward, some of the disciples and others of the more enthusiastic casting their garments before him and bursting into song, As they were crossing the Valley of Hedron on their way to the city gates, they were met by another little band of Galilean followers who had already come to Jerusalem. These came out waving palm branches and singing. Some of the men and women who had accompanied him from Bethany sang as they came:

'Blessed be he that cometh in the name of the Lord! Oh, give thanks unto the Lord, for he is good!"

From the band that had come out to meet them from the city gates came the response:

'For his mercy endureth forever.'

And again from the oncoming pilgrim band:

'Hosanna, hosanna, the Son of David! The Mighty One! The Mighty One! Son of David! . . . Hosanna, Hosanna! Blessed is the King of Israel that cometh in the name of the Lord!'

This, with various types of song and response, was a common way of greeting pilgrim bands as they came up to the great festival. The procession of which Jesus was the center began to be considerably augmented; ardent friends, towns people, curiosity-seekers, boys with their shrill voices who so quickly gather on such occasions.

Some of his disciples and friends began to take alarm. They were pleased at the reception, but they saw he was not entering the city as a conqueror. Those high in authority were not there to receive him — no, not one. As his following grew it became mostly a shouting rabble.

'Master, see what you are doing. Be careful. Be careful for your safety and for ours.' They feared that it might take on the appearance of a nationalist demonstration — for the Roman authorities had their legionaries everywhere, and they might with ruthless force quickly check it, as they had many others. They knew also that the chief priests and the Pharisees and their council had their spies posted, and that they might move with quick vengeance against such a demonstration flouting their authority, especially when they knew who the leader was. There was danger from both sides.

The enthusiastic admirers and staunch supporters of the Master fancied that he was actually to ascend the throne of David — he, son of David — and to become their King. Others in suppressed excitement thought only that something most unusual — they knew not exactly what — was about to occur. This we infer from Luke's account: 'They thought that the Kingdom of God should immediately appear.'

But in the eyes of the more respectable and aristocratic Jews, Jesus and his band of disciples and elated followers were nothing more than an ill-clad group of ignorant countrymen and hangers-on, no different from thousands of others drawn on this occasion to the Holy City. They had seen many such groups in other years.

Now, however, it began to be noised about that the prophet of Galilee and his following were come.

Nothing immediately happened. The genius of the Master again asserted itself. He dismounted from the colt, and the procession disbanded, threading itself in little groups here and there as they entered the city gate and made their way to the temple. Whatever was in the mind of the prophet of Galilee, whatever his purpose, he felt that it had been fulfilled. Everything was carefully planned on his part during these final six days at Jerusalem, and in all things he seems to have acted with a very definite precision.

We of today, partly because of the majestic music which has since been written and which is sung in the churches, get the impression that there was a great triumphal entry into Jerusalem. Evidently there was not. The occasion, however, served some purpose in the mind and the plan of the Master. Might he have fulfilled, for those who then and even more today set store by such things, the strained letter of some prophecy — Zechariah, for example: 'Thy King shall come to thee, lowly, and riding upon an ass?' Yet we can rest assured that the genius of the Master, in his great message of life, was far greater than this.

It was approaching evening when he and his disciples reached the temple, about the time of the evening sacrifice, and with all other activities ceased. The city was thronged with people. There was no place to stay, so Jesus and his little band made their way across to nearby Bethany — perhaps to the home of their friends with whom they had so often tarried.

Chapter 14
He Teaches the Great Truth

The next morning as he and his twelve stalwart followers come to the temple court, activity is at its highest: the bleating of frightened animals soon to be killed for sacrifice, with the barnyard smells filling the air; the vendors of doves hurrying here and there; traders at the concessions crying their wares; priests in their abundant and richly coloured robes hurrying about; money-changers doing a thriving business, translating specie from many different provinces and countries into the temple coin; the Master and his followers in their provincial garb pushed or jostled or importuned to buy. Possibly someone is cheated by a money changer, or perhaps some poor woman with her scanty savings is overcharged for a pair of doves — whatever the immediate occasion, the prophet of Galilee is stirred and stirred deeply.

Then in a fury he overthrows the tables of the money-changers, and turns upon the different traffickers to drive them out of the temple court. 'It is written, my house is the house of prayer; but ye have made it a den of thieves.'

At any previous time, however deeply he might have been aroused, his method would have been that of gentle admonition. Such was the nature of the man. But now a change has come. A fire and a determination seem to burn in every act.

Is it part of a plan on his part to compel those who are seeking his arrest to make it? The news of his daring quickly spreads; he must inevitably hear from the temple authorities. That day and the next he and his followers make their way through various parts of the temple, attracting, even among the great throngs, more and more attention. He boldly teaches in the temple. He denounces with increasing violence the scribes and Pharisees and priests. He discusses whatever they will with excited priests, sent to trap him. They try to make an ally of the Roman authorities that they may trap him in a civil or political indiscretion or offence. The chief priests and the scribes and the elders even follow him at times as he walks through the temple.

They are getting continually more anxious. 'And they send unto him certain of the Pharisees and of the Herodians, to catch him in his words. And when they were come, they say unto him, Master, we know that thou art true, and carest for no man: for thou regardest not the person of men, but teachest the way of God in truth: Is it lawful to give tribute to Caesar, or not? Shall we give, or shall we not give? But he, knowing their hypocrisy, said. unto them, Why tempt ye me? bring me a penny, that I may see it. And they brought it. And he saith unto them, Whose is this image and superscription? And they said unto him, Caesar's. And Jesus answering said unto them, Render to Caesar the things that are Caesar's, and to God the things that are God's. And they marveled at him.' (Mark 12:13-17)

In various ways they again try repeatedly to trap him, but again in practically all cases they are trapped themselves. Sometimes it results in jeers from the crowd standing by and listening. They are getting continually more angry and desperate and determined. Here also occurs an incident which brings a masterful teaching universal and timeless in its content — the incident of the woman taken in adultery.

An expositor takes seven pages to elucidate it — a motion-picture producer might require seven reels. The real gist is this: 'He among you that is without sin let him cast the first stone.' A closely allied law pertaining to our common life would be: He alone that is perfect has the right to judge another. And no one is perfect. Were he perfect, he still would not judge another. Anyway, to judge another it would be necessary to have all the facts running back even to generations, and these no one ever has. The Master understood. He knew. 'Go thy way and henceforth sin no more.'

Interesting things occurred one after another. His every move and act and saying seemed to be charged more than ever with: I must be about my Father's business. Everything points to the fact that he realized his end was near. Some of his most salient teachings seem directed to clarify further and emphasize his great fundamental message, which during the previous months and years he had worked so hard to deliver.

Added statements, brilliant parables, pointed back to the Kingdom and centered around it but they more and more involved something to be done, rather than something merely to be received and believed. Men believing acted and, in acting, they were saved. Merely to believe is nothing. It gets one nowhere, unless it is followed by doing. It is thus that the truth makes one free.

His observation is keen. He sees everything; and he pours out many a lesson. 'And Jesus sat over against the treasury, and beheld how the people cast money into the treasury: and many that were rich cast in much. And there came a certain poor widow, and she threw in two mites, which make a farthing. And he called unto him his disciples, and saith unto them, Verily I say unto you, That this poor widow hath cast more in, than all they which have cast into the treasury: for all they did cast in of their abundance; but she of her want did cast in all that she had, even all her living.

Another occasion, arising from the priestly group, gave him an opportunity for his greatest saying. Just what they had in mind on this occasion it is very hard to tell. A lawyer, an interpreter of the ecclesiastical code, stood up and asked the question: 'Master, which is the great commandment in the law?' Jesus said unto him, 'Thou shalt love the Lord thy God with all thy heart, with all thy soul, and with all thy mind. This is the first and great commandment. And the second is like unto it. Thou shalt love thy neighbour as thyself. On these two commandments hang all the law and the prophets.'

It seems almost as if Providence destined that this great affirmation should come during the last week of his life and ministry here. It was the most important thing of these last few days, even more important than his death; for it was primarily, we might say, to seal this fundamental thought into the thought and the life of the world that he willingly and eagerly gave his life. For our own good and our share in the good of the world we must return to it.

Time is passing, many things are happening, and the priestly authorities are getting desperate. They clearly see now that it is either his life or their authority and power — and living. They would either make a holiday of him or he would make a laughing-stock of them. The whole ecclesiastical system, with all its perquisites that it has taken years and even generations to build up, with all of its ramifications of tribute that flow in from many different sources, is being endangered.

The chief priests then ordered that he be taken and brought to them. They must have a sufficient charge, with sufficient evidence, however, and they dare not have him taken in public, lest his friends and followers and the friendly populace cry out against it and make a commotion which the Roman officials might be called upon to deal with.

They then resort to money in bargain with Judas, whom they find with an eye to business. They make a compact that he will lead them and their officers to some secret place, under cover of darkness, where Jesus may be taken and in this way avoid the risk of any public protest or tumult. Of the twelve, Judas seems the most worldly minded, the most actuated by a sense of personal gain, and the most discontented with the outcome of three years' association with the Master. The wait is not long.

Chapter 15
When a Brave Man Chooses Death

Immediately after the Passover feast with the little band, with all of its hallowed associations, he leaves the inn with the twelve, or rather now with the eleven, for one has slipped out to fulfill his compact with the chief priests. They cross over the little stream to the east of the city to the Mount of Olives.

There is a walled garden here to which the Master and his disciples seem to have been given welcome entrance by its owner, since they have visited it many times for quiet, and sometimes for sleeping at night. It is called Gethsemane, from an old olive press that stands near its entrance. The disciples notice an almost brooding solemnity on the countenance of the Master. Taking three, John, Peter and James, with him, he leaves the others at the garden gate. Going in a short distance he then leaves the three and bids them wait, watch, pray, while he goes a little farther in.

Alone he thinks and prays and seeks the light — the light that he must now follow, for he realizes that the hour of decision for him has come. His intuition tells him that the alternative is escape then and there — voluntary on his part and still easy — and survival, or remaining to meet death, death in a very short time. He realizes full well why Judas slipped out from the supper they have just had together.

He perceives that one way lie life and all it may still have for him: love, friends, continued even if restricted teaching, success. The other way lie trumped-up charges of blasphemy or sedition, abuse, public dishonour apparent failure, a cruel, torturing death.

There is still time to make his way out of the garden with his followers; slipping down the side of Olivet to the east, before long they could cross the Jordan and be safe. Or, going north, they could soon be again in their own native Galilee, among friends eager to welcome them. By being quiet for a while they would be secure. Which shall it be?

He is young; the urge of life is strong — a joy-filled life, such as his has been up to the last half-dozen days. The love of friends is strong. He knows life. He doesn't know death. The realization that has been his, the God-life within, has made life a thrilling adventure. Revealing in his teaching this truth of life to his people so sorely in need of it has but accentuated for him the joy of life. And in this great human service he has tasted true greatness.

Will not the same Father who has led him and cared for him in life, lead him and care for him if it is to be death? To be afraid, then, a coward, were inconceivable. What to do? Again the genius of the Master asserts itself.

How will his truth — the truth that will make men free, the truth which he has sought for three years to bring to his people with all the passion and driving purpose of his life — be affected by his decision? This will be the determining factor. To live for it may be well. To die for it may bring the greater gain. As has been stated, he had a superb intuitive knowledge of human psychology. Hence, 'And I, if I be lifted up from the earth, will draw all men unto me.' Hence, spoken within the week: 'Except a grain of wheat fall into the earth and die, it abideth by itself alone; but if it die, it beareth much fruit.'

Or again, was he growing weary, weary that his three years of joyfully given work hadn't produced more tangible results? Now that his popularity was waning might it be legitimate for him to consider this? Grievances, if desired and countenanced, are many. Deserted first by his own neighbours; at times questioned and misunderstood and to that extent deserted by his family and relatives; questioned and not fully understood by his best friend; deserted now by the crowd; confronted at times by dull-mindedness and contention in the twelve he had chosen and had so much depended upon; betrayed now by one, to be denied by another, and at the last to be abandoned by all (for with a peculiar intuitive sense he had seen this coming and almost within the hour had spoken it before them). In addition he is hounded now and persecuted by the leaders of his people's religion.

In the face of all this, and other things that might have come to him which he never mentioned, was he growing weary? Will the genius of the man again assert itself?

Or again, was his great enveloping vision, of the Kingdom of God that was to come and rule in the world, too slow of realization? Was the Kingdom-to-be too slow in coming through the individual? It was the individual, the individual receiving his message of the Kingdom of God within, that must multiply to numbers great enough to make the Kingdom of God here on earth. Did this realization cause the change that came about in him and result in the choice of death?

And then again — wonderful thought and hope — did he have such faith in the triumph of life over death as he has already intimated? Was it in his mind that he would arise and come again in a power and glory that would bring the establishment of the Kingdom of God here on earth; and that would be far greater than any influence he could have by staying on with this work here? That some such thing not only might but would occur, and occur shortly, even before the generation then living had passed, he fully believed. Various statements made during these last few days of his life furnish very clear evidence of it.

Whatever he might have thought, and he alone knew all that he thought, the hour for decision has come, and decide he must. One thing that stands out clearly now is this — he is no coward. Every thought and every act of his life up to the present time give clear evidence of this. To know and to do the right thing — that is what earnest, devoted thought, earnest prayer, even the prayer of supplication, are helping him now to find.

The urge of life is strong — 'Father, all things are possible unto Thee; take away this cup from me. . . .' The urge and the will to know and to do the right thing for his truth is stronger — 'Nevertheless not what I will, but what Thou wilt. . . .'

The same urge that has been with him all his life and pushed him on to give his message of life still holds him: I must be about my Father's business. And my Father's business, my brother, is to make known to you who and what you are. I and my Father are one. As I am you shall be. There is but one Principle of life. You are a worm of the dust, a poor fallen creature, only as you think you are, or as dogma may work in a stupid or cowardly mind. You are a child of God with the life, the love, the power, the glory of the Eternal in you. Only you must know it and live as such. This is my life message, my gospel, my good news, and it is for you.

By lifting your mind from your lower conception of self to the knowledge of the Divine life within you, I become your saviour, even as I would be the saviour of all men through this my truth — the truth that shall make you and all men free. You are born through this knowledge of the Spirit into the new life. The words that I speak unto you are Spirit and are life. He that heareth my word, and believeth . . . hath passed out of death into life. Through this higher knowledge of life and living in it, the Christ becomes enthroned in you as it has in me. They will kill me for this, for it is not according to their code, and it weakens their hold. . . .

The genius of the Master, so uniformly asserting itself, took his mind always away from himself, that there be no interference with his truth. 'To this end have I been born, and to this end am I come into the world, that I should bear witness unto the truth.' To this he was as true as the needle to the pole. `Is he a self-seeker, a weakling, a coward? Will he go, or will he stay?' A man really fired by the truth is never a coward, even in face of death.

Here is a man contemplating a series of situations, seeking the light, but a man. As soon as the light breaks clear and strong he will decide. He . . . It breaks. He decides. He arises. He stays. The genius of the man again asserts itself; and we never should have had any doubt as to what his decision would be.

He goes back for the third time to his disciples, some near and some at the entrance to the garden, and finds them still sleeping. It makes but little difference now, for his decision is made.

Chapter 16
Bigotry in Fear Condemns and Kills

Scarcely has he spoken with them again, when a winding row of flickering lights is seen coming up the stony pathway which he and his disciples have trodden so often. Some of the chief priests and Pharisees and their officers, other haters of 'this man Jesus,' and a considerable number of loiterers-about, in all making no small group, confront and begin to encircle him.

He knows what it means. He is ready. 'Whom seek ye?' 'Jesus of Nazareth.' 'I am he,' he replied. Then as he motions towards the disciples: 'Let these go their way.' Even the kiss of Judas isn't necessary, the sign agreed upon when he made his money compact with the chief priests.

The priestly party, with their officers and the motley crowd following them, make their way down the path across the brook and back through the city gates. The accounts differ, but one says that instead of being taken directly before the high priest who ordered his arrest, he was taken to the ex-high priest and man of dubious honesty, Annas. Why this move? The answer may be found in the fact that the chief reason why he must be put out of the way — it would simmer down eventually to his interference with the temple traffic — must not appear to the public or to the Roman authorities.

Annas, respectable, safe as a churchman, wealthy, astute, experienced, with his four sons forming a coterie, would be able to devise the most expedient maneuver. Moreover, having had other dealings with the Roman governor Pilate, who would have to sanction any charges brought against the prisoner before sentence could be carried out, he, Annas, could best devise the means of approach. What passed between him and the prisoner is not recorded, only that he was sent bound under cover of darkness to Caiaphas the high priest. A speedy call was sent for the gathering of the members of the Sanhedrin, and immediately charges were brought, or rather first devised and then brought.

The first charges and the most plausible were those of sedition. He had tried persistently to disturb the peace of the nation; he had spoken against the authority of Caesar, when all knew that they had no king but Caesar. False witnesses were hired to testify against him along these lines. They could get no agreement among them, so these charges failed.

The proceedings were exciting — desperation sometimes breeds excitement. Various attempts were made to make Jesus talk, so as to convict him from evidence out of his own mouth. He knew his legal rights and in the main kept silent. Once when the high priest asked him why he did not reply to the charges, in a quiet, clear-cut manner Jesus replied: 'If I told you, you would not believe me, nor would you let me go.'

Time is being lost. Their quarry may escape. The high priest cuts matters short and comes directly to the question in reserve. Said Caiaphas: 'Art thou the Christ, the Son of the living God?' The answer was, 'I am.' They had him put under oath. Jesus knew what that meant. He did not evade; but he made no attempt to explain to their dull and unsympathetic ears just what he meant. To make oneself equal to God or to rank with God was blasphemy in the Jewish law at that time, and was punishable by death. Caiaphas tore his garment. It was a part of their code for a high priest to tear his garment on hearing a blasphemy. The high priest then said: 'What need we any further witnesses? Ye have heard the blasphemy: what think ye?' And they all condemned him to be guilty of death.

So far so good. But the right of imposing a death sentence had been taken away from them when they came politically under the Roman rule.

It must be sanctioned by the Roman authorities. Pilate, the Governor of Judea, the local representative of the Emperor Tiberius, was reluctant to yield to the wishes of the Sanhedrin. He quickly realized that their charges of sedition were trumped-up charges. He knew practically nothing of Jesus. Hearing it mentioned that he was a prophet from Galilee, in order to find a way of escape for himself, he sent him to Herod who was the ruler of the province of Galilee, and who was in Jerusalem at the time. Herod refused to sanction the conviction, and sent him back to Pilate.

After examining Jesus privately and at length, Pilate came out and announced that he found no charges which would warrant the death penalty. He gave every evidence of wanting to be just and fair in his findings — even more than the prisoner would allow him; for he could get no help from Jesus. Twice he decided and announced to them that he would let him go. That was his own inclination and his own judgment: 'I find no fault in this man.' The desperation of the members of the Sanhedrin and their followers, now a large gathering, grew so that it turned them almost into a shouting mob.

Pilate, when he had called together the chief priests and the rulers and the people, said unto them: 'Ye have brought this man unto me, as one that perverteth the people: and, behold, I, having examined him before you, have found no fault in this man touching those things whereof ye accuse him. No, nor yet Herod: for I sent you to him; and, lo, nothing worthy of death is done unto him. I will therefore chastise him, and release him. (For of necessity he must release one unto them at the feast.) And they cried out all at once, saying, 'Away with this man, and release unto us Barabbas' (who for a certain sedition made in the city, and for murder, was cast into prison). Pilate, therefore, willing to release Jesus, spoke again to them. But they cried, saying, 'Crucify him, crucify him.' And he said unto them the third time, 'Why, what evil hath he done? I have found no cause of death in him: I will therefore chastise him, and let him go.' And they were instant with loud voices, requiring that be might be crucified. And the voices of them and of the chief priests prevailed. And Pilate gave sentence that it should be as they required, and he released unto them him that for sedition and murder was cast into prison, whom they had desired; but he delivered Jesus to their will. (Luke 23:14-25)

One can't help having a certain sympathy for Pilate. He evidently had a sense of fairness and justice. He occupied a peculiar position and he felt he must consider his own security in that position. Had he possessed the bravery, or even a mere fraction of the courage, of the man whose conviction he finally and reluctantly sanctioned, the desperate determination of the members of the Sanhedrin would have been thwarted. Had he known the real stature of the man before him, had he known what the coming ages would bring, he undoubtedly would have done otherwise. As it was, he was eventually relieved of office and recalled to Rome, and there he took his own life.

The same element of haste that had prevailed marked now the action of the priestly group; for almost immediately Jesus was led away, followed by chief priests, various members of the Sanhedrin and a varied crowd, to an elevated spot just outside the city, where executions by crucifixion, the Roman method then in vogue, were carried out. Stoning to death would have been the Jewish method that would have been used, were they still retaining their political power.

Preparations are quickly under way and the prophet of Galilee was nailed through hands and feet to the cross, Two others were executed at the same time, one an either side. Theirs was a common and insignificant offence: theft. No attention was paid to them by those present high in authority; for the thieving of these men had been petty and could not have affected their own thieving — indirect but on a much larger scale. The man they were interested to kill, had he been allowed to proceed with his enlightenment of the people, might have freed the people from the domination of the priestly class, so that their authority and their business might easily have come to an end. Good churchmen, good business men, respectable, keen, calculating, they knew it and they worked under cover.

Bigotry is a spawn of dogma that builds itself into a religious system, or rather a system of so-called religion. While preparations were under way many respectable and pious Jews, some of high authority who as a rule would scarcely hurt a fly, reviled him with various types of obscene names, struck him, and spat in his face. Honestly and righteously they did it from a sense of duty; for they were told that he was a blasphemer, and the fact that he was there under sentence to die was proof of it. They were therefore not bigots, but honest religious men upholding the sacred honour of a sacred religious institution and so serving their God so they were taught by the system, and so they believed.

The afternoon wore away and eventide approached. The soldiers on guard sat by, gambling, and one account says that they gambled for his garments. Jesus could see everything that was going on and hear everything that was being said. The same love and courage that had dominated every act of his life were manifested by him before he was raised on the cross and while life was ebbing on the cross.

When he was reviled he reviled not again. He knew the ignorance and the passions of men; but he knew equally well, if not better, the power of love, and it undoubtedly helped give him a self-contained fortitude in this final crisis of his life. He knew why he was here. He was dying for a purpose: the truth and the continuing power of his life message; and it gave him a self-mastery and a courage that undoubtedly lightened his pain.

Even here he lived his teachings. Even for his enemies, acting through ignorance, he was concerned — 'Father, forgive them; for they know not what they do.' He understood thoroughly why he was dying; it was a part of his plan sanctioned by the love and wisdom of his Father that he should give his life for the sealing of his truth. He knew even here that he would have the same care and guidance of the Father that he had always had, and that He would not desert him.

Concerning that love and care he never had had any doubt; and he had no doubt here. When he cried near the close: 'Eli, Eli, lama sabachthani,' he neither thought: nor said: 'My God, why hast Thou forsaken me?' The real meaning of these Aramaic words is: 'My God, for this end was I kept. I am fulfilling my destiny. I am dying for the truth that Thou gavest me; to this end was I born; to this end I am now come.'

And then, he cried triumphantly: 'It is finished.' Right through to the end that same faith and courage and confidence: 'Father, into Thy hands I commend my spirit.'

Chapter 17
Other Helpers of the Way-Shower

That the love and the wisdom of God were manifested in and through the Way-shower, to an unusual degree, is evident. The power of God worked through him; or rather by his living completely in the realization of the essential oneness of his life with the God-life, and opening himself trustingly to the inner wisdom, the laws through which God works were so revealed to him that he became the instrument of the power.

Frankly he said it was this creative spirit of life that he called the Father, and affirmed that of himself he could do nothing, but only as he realized the oneness of his life with the Father's life and lived fully in that realization. The Father, he says, never leaves him alone or in the dark or in need, for he seeks always to know and to do the will of the Father. It was always, though, 'my Father and your Father,' and herein lies the value of his revelation, his teaching, his life to us men on earth. Eagerly, passionately, almost desperately, we might say, he endeavours to make this known. Frankly he states the secret of his own life: 'It is not I but the Father within who doeth His work.'

Although he glories to be the teacher, the Way-shower, frankly and humbly he says, 'Call me not good, for there is only one good and that is God.' Although speaking always with authority — the authority of a teacher — he never exalted himself. Again and again he stated that he that exalted himself, as himself, in distinction from the power working within him, should be abased.

It was his experience of God first-hand that makes him the real and great teacher — that makes him speak with authority. So impressed were his hearers with the manner of his speech in this, that they often remarked concerning it. His words carried a freshness and a conviction that many times made them stand in awe, and that made many follow him eagerly.

His manner was different from that of their teachers of religion. There was never any harking back to the authority of someone or something in the past; and as to the priests of the temple, now primarily their overlords instead of ministers of religion — never a mention, except to flay and castigate them as dogmatists and self-seekers, the very opposite of what he came to portray.

They took the law, the 'wall of the law,' they took the truth of the prophets — free and independent men who opened themselves to the voice of their God — and built it into a system with innumerable hedges and observances. They said: You must believe and observe these things we tell you, or you have no religion or the benefits of religion. You must support and reverence the institution. In this way they raised the dead hand between a man and his God. They fed with stones instead of bread and demanded recognition and reverence and a price for doing it.

It was the very opposite of the teachings of the Master; and we can readily see why his righteous indignation at times flared forth. Than Jesus of Galilee, the world has perhaps known no greater enemy, ancient or modern, of religious dogmatism. Not that he opposed religious institutions — only that type which receives its system of dogma from dead hands of the past, and which would weave it into crowns to be pressed on other men's brows.

It was Emerson, he of clear-seeing mind and free and independent spirit, who said: 'If a man claims to know and speak of God, and carries you backward to the phraseology of some old mouldered nation in another country, in another world, believe him not.' And again he said:

'Yourself, a new-born bard of the Holy Ghost, cast behind you all conformity and acquaint man at first hand with Deity. . . . Nothing is at last sacred but the integrity of your own mind. . . . God is one and omnipresent; here or nowhere is the whole fact.'

Emerson's wide understanding is also shown by his saying, 'As there is no screen or ceiling between our heads and the infinite heavens, so is there no bar or wall in the soul where man ceases and God begins. . . . Ineffable is the union of man and God in every act of the soul.'

And we all know 'O friend, never strike sail to a fear! Come into port greatly, or sail with God the seas!'

Another, whose intuitive sense was more than common, independent of spirit and always open, caught the message of the Master. It was Channing who said: 'One sublime idea has taken strong hold of my mind. It is the greatness of the soul, its divinity, its union with God. . . . The greatness of the soul is especially seen in freedom of will and moral power. . . . I cannot but pity the man who recognizes nothing God-like in his own nature. . . . The soul viewed in this light should fill us with awe. . . . It is an immortal germ which contains now within itself what endless ages are to unfold. . . . It is truly an image of the infinity of God.'

His was a magnificent character, a magnificent influence in American and in English- speaking life. As we have just seen, he believed supremely in God; he knew God. He believed in the divinity of Jesus, that the Christ became enthroned and dwelt in him. But in his day he was called a Unitarian! He did not believe in the virgin birth.

He did not believe that Jesus did not have a father. But he knew history, ancient history, when it was linked with mythology. And he knew that a similar belief was quite common, and that about the nebulous time dogma began to take form, there were scores of men, well known men, who had to be accounted for in some unusual way — who had no father. Their mothers conceived and bore them through contact with, or impulse from, some mythological character, or angel, or spirit, or god. Various theories were held as to the method of contact; one of the most popular, for quite a while at least, was that it was through the ear.

Channing knew that this was held to be true of many of the Roman Emperors, of whom Augustus was a conspicuous example. They demanded such recognition and belief. He knew that there were many thousand early Christians who, because they would not publicly subscribe to it and so perjure their minds and souls, were hounded, were driven to the catacornbs, were tortured, and were put to death by those in power.

He knew that Nero and others in the imperial line demanded this belief, and were ruthless in their extermination of numberless early Christians — infidels (in their regard) who would not profess it, enemies of the existing religion, enemies of the State. Martyrs they were, almost unbelievable in their faith and their courage.

They were free minds in the sense Channing intended when he wrote: 'I call that mind free which protects itself against the usurpations of society, does not cower to human opinion, and feels itself accountable to a higher tribunal than man's.

'I call that mind free which sets no bounds to its love . . . recognizes in all human beings the image of God . . . and offers itself up a willing victim to the cause of mankind.

'I call that mind free which, conscious of its affinity with God . . passes the bounds of time and death . . . and finds inexhaustible power in immortality.'

We men and women of today should be grateful, far more grateful than we are, for the freedom, the intellectual freedom, the moral and spiritual freedom that we have. Contrast our condition with that of these early disciples and followers of the Master — the way they were persecuted and massacred for daring to think their own thoughts, and to follow and be true to their own beliefs.

And then later, when another type of Church was formed, and it grew powerful and passed into the hands of political and ecclesiastical traders for power and authority and revenue; when it was buttressed in its system of dogma which the free minds and spirits of vast numbers would not subscribe to — how they were hounded and persecuted and murdered by the thousands, by the tens of thousands!

Times and places where no man could call his mind or his soul his own, where no free mind could think and speak his thoughts without risk of seeing the pots of boiling oil, the burning pyre, or the dungeon from which perhaps he would never again emerge alive. When killings ceased, persecutions continued.

There was a time — we forget that there was — when the Bible was a closed book, concealed and kept from the people, and only such fragments let out as suited the purposes of the organization. And then the great epoch came, the uprising, the reformation when brave and courageous men seized and translated and gave it to the people — and now no man so poor but can own it and read it and interpret it for himself.

The people struggled along as best they could with their downtrodden, unlit lives. Beyond knowing that there was such a person, they knew nothing of the life, the truth, the purpose of Jesus of Galilee. They knew nothing of his realization, his own teachings, his real message —

'You shall know the truth and the truth shall make you free.' They did not know that he had lost his life by arousing the enmity of ecclesiastical leaders of the sordid type that now again prevailed.

His truth, his gospel, his good news that thrilled him and that he was inspired to give to all who would hear, had been thrust aside, side-tracked. A system embracing matters of opinion about him had been switched in its place on to the main track — and the people were told that his life and his death were for a different purpose. This better served the purpose of the dogmatists, the purpose of a close organization. Dogma has no affiliation with truth; it must be built upon something else.

The result was that the vital life-giving, life-saving religion of the Master became changed into a fear-ridden, parasitic religion about him. The forward-looking, divinely inspired, and divinely inspiring truth of the prophet of Galilee, fell into the hands of the uninspired priest, who endeavoured to relate it to a system and built a system upon it. So it started looking backward. With the eclipse of his truth came the greatest loss that the life of the world has ever known.

Will his truth, his gospel, his good news — it is all so simple, he said, if you will take it as I give it to you — come again? Will it come with a power to dominate the lives of enough individuals that through them it may yet redeem a stricken world?

Has the Way-shower been biding his time? Is his projected second coming — the spirit of his truth — in even greater power, near in the life of a troubled world? If in Christendom the great body of believers, or semi-believers, in things about him can, by the transforming of their minds and spirits, be transformed into divinely inspired, virile disciples of the Master, through an understanding and a following of his teachings, so simple as he gave them, yet so certain in their results, then it can be.

In this way, as he so longed, he may yet become the light of the world.

Chapter 18
Look Up and Drop that Load

There are three things that the Master stood for, and exemplified to a superlative degree, and that make him of such great value to men of today.

He was the in-knower; the man of courage; the man of love. His unusual sense or faculty of immediate awareness resulted in his wonderful aptitude for understanding life, and discerning the things of the mind and the Spirit as attributes of life. He knew life as Spirit, and spirit as the God-stuff of life. He knew man as spirit and spirit therefore as the God-stuff of man.

Unalterably he identified the two: God out-flowing and manifesting Himself in the life of man, and in the fullest sense the life of all in existence; man receiving, consciously receiving, and in turn manifesting the life of God. Hence Jesus' realization for himself: 'I and my Father are one.' Hence his understanding and his specific assertion: "As I am so you shall be.' And it could not be otherwise, for when he perceived and taught that God is Spirit, the Universal Spirit manifesting itself as life, then there is but the One Life, flowing out and becoming the energizing force in all things, to whose existence it gives form and substance.

For individual man consciously to realize this, enables him to become an intelligent and a mastering expression of the one Universal life. There is no sense of separation. There is no separation. There is at-one-ment — man one with his Maker, realizing and living in that true and high state.

This at-one-ment becomes effective in the life of each individual man who receives, who believes, and who lives this truth of the Master, the truth he gave the full and eager plenitude of his life to reveal, to teach, and eventually to die for. To each individual man in this way he becomes a saviour, and as he so expressly, so eagerly, and so continually taught, he cannot become a saviour, any man's saviour, in any other way.

To connect him with any scheme of salvation based upon anything different from this his truth, is to do violence to his truth, and to deny his truth is to deny him. Through this his truth he becomes the mediator, the mediator uniting man with his God.

This is in truth the atonement that becomes real and effective in its results. For one to get clearly his message, to realize clearly his truth — that one's life is from and in this one Universal life, and that one may so order and so live one's life — gives one that more abundant life which the Way- shower meant when he said; 'I am come that you might have life and that you might have it more abundantly.'

It was this truth of life which his in-knowing sense, his cosmic sense perceived, which he realized and lived and demonstrated and then made it his life mission to reveal to others, and his persistent courage and self-giving love in doing this make him indeed the great liberator of the human mind and spirit and life.

Many who heard him directly were so impressed by the genuineness and the power of his personality, and through this the genuineness and the power of his truth, that they believed; and his asserted transformation in their lives almost immediately took meaning and form. One who was his ardent follower and advocate said: 'As many as believed on him, to them gave he the power to become sons of God.'

Truth is reasonable, Truth is universal, Law is universal, hence immutable. We men of today are potential possessors of a far more abundant life than in our hurry, carrying our little loads that become big loads, we realize. In our ignorance, our rush, our fear and our worry, we inhibit the power that, working in and through us, would do the thing far better than the little self can ever do it, and enable us to live a life far more carefree.

. . . Hear me, he said, hear my word: I would become your friend, your saviour. I would save you from that sense of separateness, that sense of aloneness, which so enfeebles you. I would lift that load of care which so tires and wearies you. It is not right to go through life with such a pack. Life is for joy, and will be joyful when it is lived aright. I would help you. I long to help you. If you will hear my word, my gospel, my good news, if you will hear and live my truth and so let me help you, your darkened, uncertain, halting way will become a God-illumined way. Reach out and grasp the unseen hand waiting in love to lead you. But you must take it. . . . Look up, you are not alone. As you look up you will then straighten up — and your pack will fall away. You have thought it a part of you, a hunch on your back. God is love, waiting for you, reception and allegiance. This larger way is the real way of life. Believe me, it is true. Take my yoke upon you and learn of me, for my yoke is easy and my burden is light. My yoke is but the link linking

your life with the Father's life. My yoke is not a burden. It is the
means of lightening your burden. Life should be joyous and light,
not heavy and gloomy and fear-laden. Otherwise it is a delusion.
But believe me, life is not a delusion. The delusion is that, in trying
to live our own little lives alone through perversity or ignorance,
we cut ourselves off from the larger Universal life; we shut out the
light; we inhibit the very power that would work in and through us
for our greatest good.

My Father does not leave me alone, or in the dark, or in need,
because I seek always to know and to do the will of my Father.
And so you will find it will be in your life if you will do the same,
for He is my Father and your Father. This is that larger and more
abundant life which I have found, and which I would have you
know. . . .

Chapter 19
Love the Law of Life

The mystic or intuitive sense of the Master not only enabled him to perceive and understand God as Spirit, the universal life force of all there is in existence, but also His manifesting nature. He not only perceived God as Spirit, but also God as love — the infinite Spirit of life and power manifesting itself and acting always in and through love.

In a sense he identified the two; for he said and continually taught, God is love. That is perhaps the reason why God came to him so naturally and so habitually as Father, and why he appreciated so readily his own natural relationship therefore as son. He realized and established himself in that filial relationship with the Father.

The Father not only loves him, but he loves the Father. The Father not only loves him and works through him, but he seeks always to know and to do the will of the Father. That understanding and that attitude of complete reliance upon and complete obedience to the Father, establish the relationship of conscious union which enables him to say, 'I and my Father are one.' He not only realizes and establishes this sense of union, of oneness with the Father, but he perceives and states and teaches that this is the natural, normal life for every man, for he realizes that law is universal.

Therefore his statement and his teaching: 'As I am you shall be. I show you the way; happy are you if you follow the way.'

It is this universal Fatherhood of God that he makes, one might say, the keystone of the entire structure of his teaching. In him we live and move and have our being. All are children of the same Father, so all are brothers, all related and interrelated. No man lives or can live to himself alone. He cannot live in indifference to his fellows, and he cannot live in hate, except to his own detriment or destruction; for it is a violation of the fundamental law of life.

Love is the primal force in life. It is the building, the constructive force. Its manifestations, its products, are always beneficent. It goes always hand in hand with faith and courage and upbuilding and continual healthy growth. Its opposite hate, which engenders fear and distrust, works always as a neutralizing, destructive force. It blights and cripples and kills.

So it was for no sentimental reason that the Master gave his knowing answer to the lawyer: that the secret of life, and therefore the whole of Life, not only is, but must be, summed up as love to God and love to one's neighbour. It is simply obedience to the law of life, and its fulfillment.

It is not a matter of choice; for one cannot violate a fundamental law of life and escape the penalty of that violation. The element of choice lies in whether one would be a wise man or a fool. Through thoughts purely of self, through self-seeking and cunning, one may gain certain ends; but one loses the power of enjoyment. One may pluck the fruit; but it turns to dust in one's hands. One may gain a certain satisfaction; but one can never know what the real happiness of life is. Instead of one's life growing and expanding, it becomes dwarfed and stunted. One becomes in time an outcast from the larger life of God and one's fellow men.

Edwin Markham was seer as well as poet when he wrote:
> The robber is robbed by his riches;
> The tyrant is dragged by his chain;
> The schemer is snared by his cunning,
> The slayer lies dead by the slain.

The Master knew. When in his reply to the lawyer he said: 'And the second is like unto it, Thou shalt love thy neighbour as thyself,' he simply spoke a truth of life that is the law of life. Understanding as he did so thoroughly the oneness of life, he undoubtedly meant, love your neighbour as yourself in the sense of his being yourself — as if his life were your own life. Otherwise there could be but little sense to his statement. A man is not inclined to love his own life as such; and so 'love thy neighbour as thyself' is merely the logical sequence, the result of obedience to the law of life and therefore its fulfillment.

I am my brother's keeper, and my brother is my keeper, in the sense that our interests are mutual, and can never be otherwise. We are dependent and interdependent one on another. The law of love compelling the law of mutuality is the very ridge-pole of our social structure, of all harmonious and satisfactory life. Not strife, contention, fighting, but co-operation, under this imperious law of mutuality, gives always the larger gain.

Love, mutuality, co-operation are the way and the only way of real self-interest. We are beginning to find that this is true. But the lessons and the losses leading us to it have been frightful. A national and a world depression, such as we have been coming through, drives home the lesson, the law, that no one class can gain, no single interest, no one man, no one class can gain and get away with it alone - can prosper at the expense of all others, at the expense of the whole.

There is no such thing as the interests of 'capital' or the interests of 'labour' as such, as separate entities. Under the law of sympathy, mutuality, co-operation, their interests run parallel. To have representatives, leaders, big enough, un-self-centered enough, to know this, is the real need — and becomes the greatest asset of capital or labour.

Service, real genuine service, is, we are of late beginning to learn, the real basis of all good business, and the way of mutuality is the way of self-interest for capital and labour.

Hatred and suspicion engender fear and strife, and strife is always self-destructive. When we consider the millions, the hundreds of millions, the billions, lost on both sides through the method of strife — ignorance of the law of life — with all the financial loss to the public and all the interference with its rights, its welfare and at times its safety — when we take all this into account we conclude that the sight of a man, supposed to be a real leader, standing and beating his head against a stone wall is no longer pleasant to contemplate. The cost is too frightful. Anyway, the final settlement comes through friendly counsel. The settlement itself must be mutual if it is to be real, a lasting settlement.

The Master's way of love is the way of sympathy, mutuality, co-operation. Love thy neighbour as thyself, and esteem his business and interests as if they were thine own business and interests. Do away with the frightful costs.

And when we step from national to international relations, the Master's way of love, with its concomitants of sympathy, mutuality, respect, quite easily and compellingly becomes again the way of self-interest. Those two splendid nations, Germany and France, for how long — it seems for almost endless ages they have been fearing and hating, hating and fearing each other! Think of the hundreds of thousands, the millions of fine young lives that have been lost to these two nations. Think of the suffering. Think of the home ties broken, the waiting, the uncertainty, the fatal news, the desolation: the destruction of homes built with such loving care, from long patient work and frugal savings; the fertile soil turned into a seething hell.

Think of the billions in costs, the frightful taxes that will go on forever — or until some foreign tide of devastation repeats history and rolls in and covers them both. The longer they fight each other, the lower and the weaker become their standards of reproduction, their standards of life, and the more defenseless they make themselves against such an eventuality.

Do not suppose that history does not repeat itself, under the same laws and causes. There was a great and proud nation once. Rome was its name. Where is Rome now? There were other nations as great or greater before Rome. Where are they now? No nation is immune, no people, none.

While the law and the penalty of hate are universal, I have, for reasons, cited particularly two nations. What has been and what remains the cause of danger and disaster in connection with these two? Their leaders — civil, religious, military — did not know, or did not really appreciate, the fact that centuries ago there was a humble wandering teacher with a wonderful knowledge of life, and of the Divine in the human. In his teaching, which they have ignored or forgotten or never knew, love is the basic law of all sane and satisfactory life; love is stronger than hate; love will conquer hate and sterilize all its frightful progeny; love is not only the way of a sane, happy, human life, but is the only way of self-interest.

They may have heard something of this; but long ago a system called Christianity was built upon various speculative and mythical theories about him, with innumerable graftings from preceding heathen religion, while his own teachings, God-given, clear-cut, life-saving and civilization-saving, were denied and violated and pushed aside.

His great truth, always and still the hope of the world, waiting, as he said, to make men free, has been forgotten or soft-pedaled, and to that extent denied to the world. Will it come again? It will come again. It must come again. In the young men and women of the world lies the hope. They will not be denied. Otherwise, the flower of their generation would go into the same rotten fodder, and their splendid young bodies lie as heaps of carrion out on the fertile fields — again the victims of fear-ridden, Christless leaders.

Dogmatic Christianity does not seem able to prevent this. It seems less able today than ever. It may have to be replaced with something else. The Christianity of the Christ, actually at work in the minds and hearts of many men of different nations, would automatically push it out and take its place.

In the case of the two nations cited, for example, what assets would accrue from following the fundamental message of the Master that love is the Law of Life! What a weight it would lift from the tax burdens of the overburdened peoples! How many lives it would save! How many bodies of splendid young men!

The time may come when the right will be taken from any man to condemn others to go to the 'front,' unless he himself must go to the front. This simple requirement might transfer many a man from the class 'patriot' to the class 'coward.' And of its own motion it might even Prevent the recurrence of war.

Chapter 20
The Creative Power of Faith and Courage

That the Master was not only a teacher of courage, but he himself a splendid example of a man of courage, every thought and every act of his life attests. It took supreme courage continually to face the members and the agents of that thoroughly entrenched religious hierarchy, who became through fear the deadly enemies of both himself and his teachings. He kept right on, however, with an inner knowledge of what it would probably lead to.

This supreme courage he evoked and manifested in the garden of Gethsemane, as he viewed his fate and reached the decision that it was best to give his life for the greater good of his truth.

That is a personal courage — a man living his teachings. But the courage that means the most to the men and women of the world is the courage that would undoubtedly take first rank in his mind and heart; for it was always the element of human service that fired both his interest and his zeal. It is this order of courage that has its birth and its being in the quality, or rather the order of thought, which he had in mind when so many times he used the word faith.

No one perhaps, or certainly no one before him, had a clear understanding of the power of thought — that thought is a force, and therefore both creative and building in its effects. Our later findings, especially during the last fifty years or so, only confirm the fact of his knowledge of this, as we get it from both his words and his acts. There were those before him who had at least a partial knowledge.

'They can because they think they can.' It was the Roman poet and thinker, Vergil, who said this; he said it of the crew that in his mind would win the race.

Translating it into a statement of actual concrete fact it means: The belief and the ideal of this belief, steadily held by them, will infuse a force into and through their bodies, their very muscles, that will give them the power to win. And, said many years ago, it agrees thoroughly with the best that we are finding in our modern science and psychology.

This was said but a few decades before Jesus, the greatest teacher of the power of thought that the world perhaps has ever known. Filled with potency are his continually repeated sayings and his direct teachings concerning the power of the moulding and creative process of thought — in the form of faith.

Thoroughly he understood that thought is a force. Intuitively he understood it, and gaining a first-hand knowledge of its laws and using it to a supreme degree himself, he then proclaimed its vital creative and building power to others. Otherwise he never could have said — and repeated — those remarkable things about faith. 'According to your faith be it unto you,' occurs in this or in similar form time and time again.

Faith, in the sense that he used it, and the sense that we must understand it today if it is to become a force — a creative and moulding force — in life, is but a positive, clear-cut type of thought, which, clearly pictured, held to and kept watered with expectation, becomes creative in its action. It makes all effort positive, dynamic, constructive; just as fear — its opposite — and fear's attendant forebodings weaken, neutralize, and finally defeat all effective effort, all accomplishment.

There seems to be a law — there is a law, the truth and the force of which we are, as it were, just beginning intelligently to grasp. It can be stated in this form: There is something in the universe that responds to brave, intrepid thought. The Power that holds and moves the stars in their courses, sustains, illumines and fights for the brave and the upright. Courage has power and magic in it.

To form one's ideal, clearly to see it, and then to make the start, is the first essential of all attainment and achievement. To take captive the best things in life, we must proceed always through the channel of brave, intrepid thought. He who knows the power of the forward look — the silent, subtle building power of faith and hope and courage — realizes that unforeseen helps will spring up all along the way, for him who makes the start, who determines to arrive and who works true to the pattern.

There is perhaps no trait that more people in the world today, right down in their hearts long for — eagerly long for — than the quality of courage. Every individual has his problems. There is no one who has not. Life is not conceivable on any other terms.

It was Shakespeare's keen vision and graphic power of expression that gave us the memorable and suggestive thought: 'Our doubts are traitors, and make us lose the good we oft might win, by fearing to attempt.' The start is not made; and with no start there can be no arriving, no achievement, or the innate joy that comes from achievement.

The initiative lies always within ourselves. There are helps, both within and without, which stand ready to respond to the vision and the call of every brave, clear seeing, and determined man and woman. The springs of power are all from within, and through this channel we can make contact with sources of power, or the Source of Power, that tremendously augments our own efforts.

Wonderful statements in this realm of thought have come to us from some of the early Hebrew prophets, many showing great inspiration, some great beauty of phrase.

To one there came: 'And thou shalt hear a word behind thee, saying, This is the way, walk ye in it, when ye turn to the right and when ye turn to the left.' To another there came: 'There is a spirit in Man: and the inspiration of the Almighty giveth him understanding.' To another:

'The Lord thy God in the midst of thee is mighty.'

We have become so used to some of these sayings through familiar association, that we are apt to lose sight of their reality. If we looked at them in a more matter-of-fact and commonsense way, we would get a great deal more out of them. Much of their value is lost, unless we recognize them as statements of facts in connection with great fundamental laws, and translate them into working facts or forces in our common everyday shall we say bread-and-butter lives.

With their minds always open to the voice of their God — Jehovah — these early prophets made it possible for the higher inspirations, the higher revelations of truth and power, to come to them.

They did have contact with the Divine, and the Divine life and power made itself manifest to and through them. The result is that here and there the Old Testament portion of our Christian Bible contains some of the greatest statements of practical philosophy, of mystical and religious thought, embodied at times in arresting beauty of form, that can be found anywhere in the literature of the world. The quiet of their life and surroundings made this type of inspiration and revelation easier and more natural for them, perhaps, than for the great majority of us today. But our need of it is just as great. Shall we say, it is greater.

The thing for us to remember primarily is this: The laws are the same now as then. If we take time to find, to know, to observe them, the results will be the same with us as with them.

One of those earlier prophets said something that revealed his grasp and his understanding of a certain law, which should make every man and woman and child among us today sit up and take notice: 'Thou shalt decree a thing, and it shall be established unto thee.'

If there is truth in this statement, then there is a force which we possess and which can be so used that as the cause it produces the effect — 'it shall be established unto thee.'

Slowly we have been coming upon the fact that thought is a force, and whether or not we realize it fully yet, it is the great building force, and therefore power, in our lives.

As we think, so we become. Such is the law. This is why we are at last finding that the life always and inevitably follows the thought.

There is no more fundamental law of life. Old as the world, but to be filled ever with fresh meaning for each individual is the truth: 'As a man thinketh in his heart, so is he.' This part is but the cumulative effects of his prevailing life thoughts.

There is a positive, constructive, success-bringing type of thought, and there is a negative, destructive, failure-bringing type or order of thought.

It was primarily of the former that the Master had so much to say. Some of his statements of its power would be almost unbelievable were it not for the fact that he had such a supreme aptitude, such a unique power, for discerning the things of the mind and the spirit.

He uses over and over again in this connection the word faith. 'According to your faith,' said he, 'be it unto you.' And again, 'If you can but believe, all things are possible to him that believeth.' To these and almost identical statements he gives dynamic utterance time and time again.

When he used the word 'faith,' he practically in every case used it in the sense of 'thought.' He never used it in the sense of having faith in, or believing in, some thing or system, for he himself taught no system. The truth of the laws of life was his sole interest and purpose and concern in his life mission of becoming the light-bearer for other men.

And faith, in the sense in which he in practically all cases uses the term, is nothing more or less than a clear-cut, positive type of thought which, set into operation and held to, becomes dynamic and formative in its operations.

It is because he understood that thoughts are forces, and are continually creating or moulding conditions, each according to its kind, that he could speak so positively and frequently of the power of faith. We are, as it were, just beginning to understand the real, vital truth of these sayings, just beginning to catch up with him.

This law of the continually creative and building power of thought is, as I have said, in a sense the most fundamental law of life, so far as conduct and achievement — or lack of achievement — are concerned.

We are now learning that when a man's mind is lifted up, his whole estate — body, spirit and all of his affairs — is lifted up. All successful men are men of great faith; and in them this positive, constructive type of thought, working always and unceasingly as a creative force, is clothing in material form that which at first was but the idea, the vision.

It is necessary, though, that we not only get but keep the vision. In our modern kind of life we are so apt to allow ourselves to become enmeshed with things, and so often with things trivial compared with the great facts and verities. We allow ourselves to get mentally, nervously, and thereby physically, depleted — fagged out, below par — through noise, commotion, motion. This we do to a degree by going to too many places, keeping too many social engagements, staying up too late at night, indulging in excesses of various sorts which rob us of the healthy balance nature demands and will have if any life is to be happy and normal and contented.

It is when we become tired and overtaxed and run down that we allow fear and worry the more easily to enter and dominate and the dark and doleful picture to present itself. It is then that we begin to lose our grip, that our vision becomes distorted, that we lose faith and courage and the never-say-die spirit.

Because of this so many men, good men, among us commit suicide, victims, when they should have been masters, of circumstance. Discouragement creeps in and gradually assumes control, and the game is up.

How little our big things become! How little some of our supposed big men become, how impotent, and often how utterly insignificant, when a great economic crisis arrives and they are compelled to stand out in their true form: temporarily rich in things, but pygmies in mental and spiritual possessions. True it is as Emerson said: 'Thus do all things preach the indifference of circumstance. The man is all.'

It is time we begin to take stock, for the safety of our social structure, as well as for the safety, the integrity, the peace and happiness of our individual lives. Through putting ourselves more fully in harmony with the laws of life, we become more fully masters of the forces of life. To do this we must take more time and opportunity to know their laws. We must become better 'listeners.'

There is no practice in life perhaps that can be productive of such good as the habit of taking a little time each day in quiet — alone — to make ourselves open and receptive to that inner guidance and power which are the heritage of every man and woman who will create the conditions whereby they can manifest themselves. This practice is of supreme value in making and keeping our connection with the infinite Spirit of life and power which works in and through all — the life of all — in the degree that we do not inhibit it. We inhibit too much. We do not give sufficient time to the 'Inner Light.'

This is true prayer. Prayer is active, sincere desire, followed by quiet receptivity, and then by direction and power and realization. That able industrialist, Henry Ford, once said to a friend:

'We pray, we do things for the good of men and women, but we do not properly relate ourselves to the Great Enveloping, Permeating Spirit.'

The Way-shower set us a great example. He took himself continually to the quiet place, in order to keep his connection with the great permeating life — 'the Father,' as was his term. He found, and we will find, that this is the true source of direction and power.

All around us men are learning, more than ever before, the power of faith and hope and courage; and in the face of severe handicaps and discouragements, many are learning in a telling way the truth that a man may be down, but never out — unless he thinks he is. Taking heart then with the day, they begin again and turn what otherwise would be inevitable failure into success and achievement and the joy that comes from achievement - if it is achievement worthwhile.

Chapter 21
How His Truth Started and then became Distorted

Immediately following the official killing of Jesus, the Light-bearer to his people, is the account of the resurrection. It is so familiar to all that it will not be dealt with here. Our concern is primarily the life of the Master, and this for the value of his great life message to the world. Almost immediately after his going, departures from his own message of truth, and thereby distortions, began. These were made more or less innocently at the time, because his immediate followers were confronted with such absorbing occurrences and experiences.

His great concern, greater than life itself, was the giving and the spreading of his great truth that would give his people freedom in a larger life: his gospel of the Kingdom of God. As it came so clearly to him he gave it freely and untrammeled; hence the overlords of his, the Jewish, religion, fearing for themselves and the institution through the spreading of his truth, and growing through their bigotry to hate him personally, killed him. The common people, his own people, who heard him gladly and followed him so eagerly, unquestionably deplored this; but they could not help themselves.

In delivering his truth and getting it established in the world he did not depend upon numbers; he did not depend upon an organization. He probably never thought of one, for he gave no instructions or direction along that line to his few followers. His observation of such organization, in the ecclesiastical group that killed him, possibly gave him warning against this. Anyway, we know that he made no effort to establish any organization, or, as we say, a Church.

A Church came into being later but was so far as we know neither directed nor sanctioned by him. It is a help for us not to forget that Jesus was a Jew. His mother was a Jewess and his father was a Jew. John the Baptist, his cousin, whom he esteemed and whose work he valued so highly, was a Jew. All of his twelve disciples, as far as we know, were Jews. Practically all of his followers before and for some time after his death were Jews. The seventy to whom he gave his simple directions to go forth and to spread his gospel of the Kingdom of God were Jews. They and the twelve, or later the eleven, following his example, carried his message either to groups out in the open, or to the congregations assembled in the synagogues, humble or mere pretentious as they found them.

At first there was but very little difference between the beliefs of these groups and the message of his followers, as they carried it to the Jewish communities already established — the congregations of the synagogue. That the Messiah had already come was the message at first. The aim and purpose was to prepare as many souls as possible to believe in the risen Jesus; and to prepare them for the 'second coming' which they uniformly believed would be in a very short time. The great majority, however, preferred to remain true to their Jewish traditions. So in this way a new sect of Judaism, the followers of the Nazarene, arose in Jerusalem and in Galilee. It was not a new religion.

Then outside, Hellenised Jews, who had had a larger contact with and outlook upon life, began to be attracted to the new sect. The addition of these and a few Gentiles here and there and the burning zeal of fresh leaders, combined to make a noticeable growth in this new Jewish sect.

They began then to seek members outside the Jewish fold. One of the first missionaries to preach to people outside Jewry was Philip, a Hellenised Jew. Driven from Jerusalem by persecutors of the sect of the Nazarenes, he carried their mesaage up and down the country. He established himself at Caesarea to the north and made it the center of his work for many years.

A second apostle and missionary to accept Gentiles into the fellowship of the Nazarene was Peter, who began but a short time after the death of Jesus to preach the risen Jesus and his early return, right in Jerusalem itself.

Then came Paul, formerly Saul of Tarsus, at one time persecutor of the Nazarenes, now converted, whose ardent enthusiasm in spreading the gospel of the new sect made him known as the 'great missionary.' His great ambition to carry the new gospel outside Jewry to the Gentiles caused him to become known especially as the apostle to the Gentiles. His ardent and long-continued work prevented the new gospel, as it developed and spread, from becoming merely a new, even if influential, Jewish sect.

It was at Antioch, a Syrian city, that the gospel of the second coming was preached with such fervour and drew so many non-

Jews that its adherents broke away from the synagogue and became quite independent, with a religion of their own. They called themselves Christians. They were the first to be so known. We see here both the Greek and the Hebrew connection. Their term, Christian, came from the Greek word, Christos, equivalent to the Hebrew word, Messiah, and means, 'Anointed One.'

The accounts of those exceedingly interesting and at times adventurous missionary journeys of Paul, with his companion Barnabas, refer often to their carrying on their work in and through the Jewish synagogues which they found already established almost everywhere they went. Others then began to spread the gospel of the new sect of the Christians.

We are told that before either Paul or Peter went to Rome there was a little Christian center already established there. It is interesting to follow the facts then, to learn that the early Christian Church, the Church of the disciples, was never founded as such, but grew in this natural way out of and had its first home in the Jewish synagogue.

When Jesus gave his instructions to the twelve and later to the seventy, as he sent them out to spread his gospel of the Kingdom of God and to heal those who needed help, he did not, so far as we know, tell them to form any organization, or even to go to any already formed.

The carpenter teacher of Galilee was a layman, never a churchman. His was a larger, a universal, consciousness and purpose; therefore his greater power and influence. He became a churchman only through appropriation on the part of others. It was not so pronounced in the few earlier years, however, so far as distortions of his own message were concerned. The simple statement of belief or creed of these early Christians was: faith in God the Father, and His Son Christ Jesus, and love of the brethren.

They were mostly simple folk imbued by a strong community spirit, and held things in common. There was equality of rank in their meetmgs. Later the office of Elder arose in the individual congregation, and that of Bishop in connection with groups of congregations. Through the zeal of the apostles and missionaries the new faith began before long to spread rapidly. The Roman authorities took alarm and began to persecute as we have already seen.

But Rome was even then declining and the people were getting so little from their own religion that many of the well-to-do and influential sought the new religion. At first it was embraced primarily by the poor and humble people. As it came under the Gentile, and especially the Greek and Roman, influence it became rapidly more speculative in its form, and more intricate in its organization. There remained but little of the simple but vital teachings of the prophet of Galilee as he gave them. The metaphysical disputants, in their efforts to define and explain and build an organization, pushed these so completely aside that they became as good as lost. As time passed, the Roman organization grew so influential that in the early part of the fourth century the Emperor Constantine, seeing that he might use it in a political way in entrenching himself against his enemies, made it the official religion of the empire. All persecutions then ceased. This was in 324.

Already their metaphysical speculations and formulations had brought about dissensions and divisions, which gave promise of disrupting the organization. Constantine, to secure unity again for his political support and safety, called, in 325, the first great council, at Nicea, at which, after a great deal of bitter wrangling and fighting, the Nicene Creed was formulated.

There was never any unanimity of opinion, but finally one of the two bitterly contending factions won. This conclave was to determine primarily the nature, and more particularly the inner nature, of God by vote; also the real relation to Him of the Son. After many stormy sessions, of which the less said now perhaps the better — as for example when Arius, the chief and noted leader of one of the two factions, got up to speak, Nicholas of Myra struck him a blow in the face — the votes were finally counted and what was to be known as the Doctrine of the Trinity emerged.

The decision was that God was three persons, fully distinct but not separate: Father, Son, and Holy Ghost - but one God. No one has ever understood it; and it has been the source of endless wranglings and divisions ever since. It was so empty of value, possibly so inconsequential in his mind, that the 'Son' never concerned himself with it. It shows, however, what theorizing speculation will do.

Later when ambitious ecclesiastics of Constantinople and Rome effected the great schism which divided Christendom into two bodies, the Greek and Latin Churches, it was caused by disagreement in connection with one word, the Latin word filiogue, meaning 'and the Son.' To this day they are still apart. The ecclesiastics in their rivalry and hatred wrangle, and the people suffer. They take the prophet of Galilee from the cross and speculate and try to explain and relate him; an enigma takes form — their formulation — and in the process his own great life teaching is emasculated and denied to the world, at least through the creeds of the high towering system that they build. One of our most authoritative historians of religion and the Church, dealing with this first conclave of Nicea and then with several others that followed to the year 451, writes:

'Over three hundred bishops, and many hundreds of priests, deacons, and acolytes, gathered at Nicea. They were for the most part zealous believers, or disbelievers, in the doctrine of Arius. For the first time the Mediterranean world saw vividly displayed that bastard form of faith, dogmatic conviction, which Europe was fated to inherit from Greece, and to suffer from for so many centuries. One frenzied sect was ready to go to the stake for their belief that God the Father and God the Son were Homoousioi, and the other for the belief that they were Homoiousioi. Even now, in nearly two thousand years, the world has hardly yet discovered that they were only attempting to measure the most unfathomable of facts with formulas and criticisms adapted to no higher purposes than those of a deplorably decadent school of grammarians. Let us dispose in a few words of what the Church did establish as its creed by the operation of its early councils, so as to leave as soon as possible a subject so humiliating to human intelligence. . . .

'But why dwell on these dogmatic dissensions when the fundamental point, after all, was that the peasant of Galilee, whose speech was Aramaic, whose mind was so simple and direct, would never have recognized in these subtleties, these frantic death struggles of the moribund Greek intellect, the teaching which he attempted to set before mankind. All we need dwell on these creeds for is to see in them a certain landmark, the end of certain well- defined phase. With them, the formative period of Christianity closes, and the religion has become rigidly constitutionalized.'

We are dealing with these matters very briefly, and leaving them now as quickly as possible for a specific purpose; and we are dealing with them entirely from an historical standpoint, for practically all forms of religion in Christendom today — Greek, Roman, and Protestant — have had their common origin. A few devout people, in their concern lest any changes be made, speak of our 'great historic creeds.' There is no such thing, at least to which the word great can be rightly applied, except great in obscurantism.

The question that must be faced today is: Do we want this system of Christianity handed down to us by these speculative ecclesiastics of a totally different age — a system brought about by their attempts to explain and then formulate a system about the Christ of Galilee; or do we want those vital life-giving teachings, the religion of the Christ of Galilee, which he, perceiving so uniquely and clearly, laboured so devotedly to convey and leave in the life of the world?

In the minds of the thinking young men and women of today there is no question. Upon them will depend the future continuation of what we term Christianity. It is a decision that can now be neither dodged nor delayed.

Chapter 22
The Truth that Must Save Christianity

We are face to face today with a condition different from any in our history. We must realize it. Thinking men and women, devout men and women are asking: What's the matter with Christianity? Young men and women keen in truth-seeking, with life before them and longing for the best in life, are asking: What is Christianity? They constitute a mighty potential force outside and independent of Christianity, or to be won to it and swell its ranks.

If they are told it is a life to be lived, vitalized and beautified and divinely socialized through the simple fundamental message of the Master, the Man Who Knew, they will be drawn to it. If they remain of the opinion that it is a system of belief, an intricately formulated system hoary with age and impotent because inadequate for our present-day needs, delivered to us by the dead of the past who in their eagerness to explain the Master forgot the message so that it never found statement as the dominating factor in any creed and in most cases not even a mention, then they will not be drawn to it.

There is something in the first view so life-building and so necessary as a help in satisfactory, happy, and therefore successful life, that, rightly perceived and presented, it will draw and attract the young men and women of today. There is no longer any appeal in the other conception, in the face of present-day knowledge and facts. To morons, yes. To thinking young men and women, no. They cannot be interested and they will have none of it; and therein lies a mighty loss.

I said but recently to an outstanding forward-looking minister of one of our churches, who possesses an unusual appeal and magnetic force for young people: 'Our churches — Christianity — today are facing a very critical condition. Their statements of belief, their speculative statements about the Master inherited from the past, no longer interest our thinking young men and women. Some of the things the old creeds contain seem to them not only inconsequential but even untrue. They do not fit with present-day knowledge.

'In a few years from now the majority of those in our churches will be gone. If their places are not taken in sufficient numbers by this on-coming, clear-seeing, truth-loving, fear-free generation, then the churches' power as an agency for righteousness mighty and prevailing — to say nothing of their ability even to carry on — ceases. The fact must be faced and the quicker it is faced the better.'

'You are right,' he replied, 'and the bulk of my fellow ministers with whom I come in contact are thinking and saying the same thing.'

The necessity of the re-statement of their articles of creed in forms of present-day truth — as life and action — is no longer open to doubt. It must be a statement brief, simple, and clear cut, built upon the Master's fundamental truth as a way of life, and not a series of statements primarily to explain him or to inculcate any theories or beliefs about him. There is where the mischief has been done. There is where or, rather, why his truth has been so emasculated. There lies the cause of all of the contentions, the fights, the divisions — and the weakening of Christianity.

I sought my friend's experience and views arising primarily from his unusual contact with the younger generation, for aid in writing a book — this book. I said to him: 'An author in preparing a book, a book of serious and, he hopes, helpful content, writes it naturally with the purpose of reaching the largest number of readers. He doesn't want to alienate, and he doesn't want to fail to show, due respect for the beliefs of others. At the same time I feel that he should be absolutely fearless in dealing with truth in his statements of present-day facts and conditions as he sees them. I have given the matter careful thought for a number of years. I am now positive that certain things should be said and without any mincing of words, or soft-pedaling of facts. There is a critical condition that must be faced quickly, and should be helped, not by way of destructive thought from any source, but with every sincere effort at constructive accomplishment.

'My admiration for our churches, for the fine work, helpful work that their ministers have done, outside their pulpit utterances, and which the world at large doesn't know and doesn't at all fully appreciate, is so great, that I long to see them bridge, and successfully bridge, the chasm which lies immediately ahead. There is no finer body of men, no more self-sacrificing and useful and helpful in our country, than the great body of ministers in our various churches. The great bulk of them is forward-looking, eager to present the truth, the Master's truth of life. They need to be less hampered. They need help. . . .'

'There,' interrupted my friend, 'you have touched the point. We do need help. You are right, absolutely right. Say the thing that you feel needs to be said. Say it boldly — don't hesitate. Our councils are slow moving — too slow for the good of the Church and the greater good that it might do. You as a layman and with no shackles can say things that we cannot say so well, although some of us may feel them just as keenly. To get the fresh and vigorous blood of youth into our churches is one of our greatest needs — for their help and their work, for their thought and their influence in rejuvenating, or one might be bold enough to say, reforming Christianity.'

Therefore I would say to any young person, whether he is emphatic or indifferent or antagonistic toward Christianity, that our churches are guided by these fine progressive men, eager to do the best they can, eager for the comradeship of young men and women who will come in and help them. Do not be indifferent to this fact. You can, if you will, find such a center. You will find such a man. Go — and know him and help him. In doing your part in connection with such a center, already established and needing support, you may find a comradeship with him and a companionship with the others beyond your wildest dreams.

In this way also you will make a natural home and environment for your children for which as time passes you and they will be very grateful. Then by the very beauty of the truth and the life that they sense, without coercion on your part or sanctioned coercion on the part of anyone, as it should always be in matters of religion and belief, they will come to natural acceptance of membership in and allegiance to such a home of the spirit. It may possibly save you from many a period of uncertainty — and even of heartache.

Time marches on. Truth marches on. The indifference of what we term Christianity to this fact is almost astounding. This made not such vital difference in the past, though a great loss was sustained. Today, however, is a different day.

There is now available a vast amount of research in connection with the methods of the institutions of the past. Fear no longer holds. There is free research and free thinking. The honest search for truth leads men and women of today to the conclusion that no institution, whatever its self-constituted claims in the past, has or should have any rightful claim or hold on any free man or woman, or any child.

Things today move quickly. We are in an era of change. Old things, old systems are breaking up — sometimes almost over-night. We must be on the alert. Change is in the air everywhere — even revolution. Change is inevitable.

How much wiser though to see and to act in time, that it be or-derly, evolutionary revolution rather than a frenzied, destructive revolution which indiscriminately pulls down the good in conjunc-tion with effete parasitic organizations of reaction that, no longer serving an adequate human purpose, should be pulled down.

In the main, churches are ready to adapt themselves, but on the other hand there are the institutions of dogma interested less in the people because now, as in the past, they are more interested in their self-preservation and in evading or fighting, as it arises, all new truth which exposes the weakness of their structure or the falsity of their original foundation. An institution of dogma defends itself not by, but against, new truth; hence it cannot draw and cannot have the free allegiance of the thinking young men and women of today — this different day.

Chapter 23
How His Truth Compels Allegiance

If the Master's truth comes with a renewed life into the world, and especially in organization form, it: will come primarily through the young men and women now entering the stage of action. They are of a truth-loving generation, thinking, searching, who quickly distinguish between truth and custom, truth and system. It is primarily in and through such young people that the hope of the Master must lie.

Youth is ever open to truth; and truth is ever young. Religion must be forever open to the flowing present with its continually unfolding truth, or it stagnates and cannot naturally and readily attract the young. That changes of conception and statement and methods must come and are brewing, no thoughtful person can have any doubt.

One may easily imagine the Master in conversation with an eager, clean-minded, clean-souled youth of today — and glad of such a hearer to whom he could give an epitome of his mind and purpose, and still more of his observations, that they might be carried by him on to others of his age and kind. Certainly it would be of great interest and value to the young man. The eagerness of youth today to get at the truth of things, especially of life and religion — of religion that may be of some value to life — would make the Master just as eager to embrace the chance of such a conversation. It would be in such thorough keeping with his accustomed methods while here.

As it was to Philip, one of his chosen disciples, that on a memorable occasion he gave a distinct message distinguishing between the flesh and the spirit, the symbol and the truth, so let us say that the name of the youth with whom he talks today is Philip. And let us suppose that Philip says eagerly: 'Those wonderful sayings of yours of the power of faith, they are almost beyond belief, and so few of us really comprehend them. How can they be true?'

'You of your day,' replies the Master, 'are just coming upon one of the greatest facts of life: that thoughts are forces, always creating. Faith, is but a positive, clear-cut type of thought. Held to, continually watered with expectation, it becomes creative in its action.

Old as the world is the truth: as we think, we become. It is the law. We must sit as master at the helm: otherwise we drift, drift, drift. Thought is our sole possession. Prayer and faith and communion all come through the channel of thought. We must not only use it, but use it right. Courage comes through this type of thought.

'Faith and courage, or shall I reverse them, courage and faith, are, I say, but clear-cut types of thought that are continually working along the lines that we are going. If not, what sense would there be in what long ago I said, "According to your faith be it unto you?" What right had I to say — "If thou canst but believe, all things are possible to him who believeth?" I have the right because thought is a force — a subtle, silent force — always creating and drawing conditions around us, in accordance with the nature of the thought that we entertain and live with.

'We have it then in our own hands,' says Philip, 'to determine exactly what our lives are to be?'

'Yes,' replies the Master. 'Search as you will, you will find no law more fundamental than that the life always and inevitably follows the thought. But come, it is of the Kingdom that we shall talk.'

'Yes,' says Philip, 'and how I long to understand aright.'

'Know,' continues the Master, 'that there is but the One Life, the Father, in whom we live and move and have our being. The Life, the power that holds and moves the stars in their courses, is the Life, the power that is in you. Only, you must realize it, and live always in this consciousness. God is spirit — the spirit that is yours. Look within, realize the Divine Centre within you — the Christ within. This is my revelation of the Kingdom. When I said. "I am come that you might have life, and that you might have it more abundantly," what did I mean? I said, "God is spirit," and "the Kingdom of God is within you." I meant that the Infinite Spirit of Life that is behind all, working in and through all, is the Life that is in you. As you realize this and live continually in this consciousness, you establish yourself in a conscious manner.

'You make the condition whereby you become an ever-increasing center of creative power. So my repeated injunction, "Seek ye first the Kingdom of God, and all other things shall be added unto you," means: realize the Divine Life, the Divine Centre within you, and you make the condition whereby the God-life works in and through you, by way of augmented direction and power. This is what I intended by my saying, "The Father in me and I in the Father," and, "As I am so shall you be." This is the secret, the reason, of my greater insight and power — as it must be of every man's.

'It might be called "The Power of Silent Demand" — the recognition and intelligent use of a force which is an inherent faculty of every mind that realizes its life as one with the Universal Life. This, moreover, is now being understood and effectively used by men and women in increasing numbers. An older prophet sensed it when he said: "Thou shalt decree a thing, and it shall be established unto thee." And so do you see what I meant when I said, "I am come that you might have life, and that you might have it more abundantly" — that this greater abundance of life becomes yours when you identify your life with the God-life within you?

'In this, and in my reply to the lawyer, you have my entire revelation and message to the world. The lawyer asked an honest question: "Master, which is the great commandment in the law?" And I replied, "Thou shalt love the Lord thy God with all thy heart, and with all thy soul, and with all thy mind. This is the first and great commandment. And the second is like unto it: Thou shalt love thy neighbour as thyself. On these two commandments hang all the law and the prophets."

'With this the truly inspired ones, the prophets, seers, and saviours of all religions agree; as also that countryman of yours who had such a keen insight in separating the wheat from the chaff, your own sainted Lincoln, when, in his inspired answer to the question why he had not allied himself with a religious organization, he said, "When any church will inscribe over its altar, as its sole qualification of membership, the Saviour's condensed substance of both Law and Gospel, that church shall I join with all my heart and soul." And in this he prophesied what will in time become the qualification for membership in every real church in Christendom. Here lies not only the whole duty of man but the essence of all religion which is the consciousness of God in the mind and the soul of man.

'And how easy it is to understand the significance of "Love thy neighbour as thyself" when we once know that we are all partakers of the One Life, the same Father, and hence are all brothers. Love is the great cosmic law of all advancing and satisfying life, the law that brings order out of chaos, the law that becomes the solvent of the riddle of life. All human relations await the capitalization of love, sympathy, mutuality, and their resultant, co-operation, to make them that splendid thing they can and eventually must be.'

'It would actually mean then Heaven on earth, and the men and women of all nations would be the gainers?'

'Yes, Philip; when men and women are wise enough to know and eager enough to follow this law, this Way of Life, a new life is born in each, and a new world order comes in. And when, and only when, this is done, will this your world be changed from the rule of the tooth and claw of the jungle, with its periodic fields of carnage, into the paradise, the kingdom, it must and shall be.'

'I know now,' says Philip, 'that it is true.'

'It is true not because I say it. I say it because it is true. The power of love is the primal force of the universe. The men and the nations that do not understand it march in ceaseless columns to their own destruction.'

As Philip sits with rapt attention, and thinking of himself, he asks: 'What about the sinner?'

'For struggling and seeking men and women, for the sinners and the care-encumbered men and women, I always had pity — infinite pity and love. The only ones I ever condemned were those I spoke of as scribes and Pharisees and hypocrites. They were those who would take the truths of the prophets and the inspired ones and, interested in themselves and their own systems rather than in the essence of the truths, would weave them into thorny crowns to press on other men's brews.

'And so today, as through the ages, the enemies of my truth and my cause — the hinderers — are those who conjecture and build systems about me, but who fail to keep my commandments, to do the things I have said to do, and to pass them on in simple purity to a sorrowing, fearing, and half-living world.'

'Oh, had I but known this — what your real message to the world is — how different my life would have been, and how different it would be today!'

'You have suffered,' replies the Master, 'but you have great love. It is because of this, and your longing to know the truth which makes men free, and which makes their life full, joyous and abundant, that I am glad to talk with you. My message is this message of the Kingdom. Find this inner Kingdom. Live in it. And then, as I said, do not worry about your life. Take it, and find in it peace and power. Neglect it, miss it, and you will continue in fears and forebodings, in weakness of mind and of spirit — and its resultant weakness of body.'

'What about your death being a substitution, a ransom for the sins of the human race?'

'Do you mean before or since my time? We know now that vast millions lived on the earth before I came. But in either case it was all news to me. Otherwise I would have said something about it during my life and ministry here. It was founded upon a mythical, an imaginary, occurrence that you know now never took place. It was founded upon the imagined and alleged fall and consequent degradation of the human race. I knew nothing of it in my time. Be that as it may. My revelation and entire teaching were exactly the opposite— not the natural sinfulness and degradation, but the divinity, of the human soul. All are sons of God and God is love, not anger and as such demanding an early Jewish conception of a sacrifice and of an atonement for an error or a sin, especially one that the individual never committed.

'That such a thing could be believed and made to enslave so many people mentally and spiritually is astounding. That it persists in even a few minds yet, in the light of my teachings, and especially when combined with your present-day knowledge, is even more so. The vast amount of money made from benighted, fearful people, through the ages and strangely enough even now, in dealing in my body and my blood, is amazing. But as fear and ignorance go, the truth that I taught will grow: that God is love and as a loving Father longs always for the son's return, longs for him to repent and turn again to His love and care. Read now again my parable of the Prodigal Son. Why did I give it? I realized that so many have need of this same light.'

'Why,' asks Philip, 'hasn't the world this wonderful truth, which seems now so simple, after all these years?'

'Men are divided, and have at times grown even to hate one another in their divisions, because they were unable to agree in theories about me, mere matters of opinion — things that do not matter — while they miss the one great thing that does matter, the truth that I brought to the world. This has fallen upon deaf ears. They do not do as I said. They do not keep my commandment. They do not seek the inner Kingdom that brings everything else in its train. They do not find the Christ within. They do not love one another. The result is fear, fear everywhere, discontent, want, envy, jealousy, strife — and periodic war and world disruption.'

'I shall bless the day,' says Philip, 'when we shall understand, so that it will not be so hard for you.'

'Yes, at times, my heart bleeds — for I would be the Saviour of men, by saving them from their lower conceptions and selves, and lifting their minds and spirits up to that Divine image and heritage which is theirs. But my great joy is in the rapidly increasing numbers all over the world, who are now getting my real message, and the wonderful Life that unfolds in them with the getting. And when enough get it, then a new world comes in.'

'If I can but keep this vision,' says Philip, enraptured, 'and live this life, and can even to a humble degree impart it to others . . .'

'You will, Philip, for I feel that now you understand. Always remember, then, that I gave summary of my life and my revelation to the world in my reply to the lawyer, when I said that the whole of life is love of God, and love and service to the neighbour. From this all else flows.

'Love to God is realization of the Divine life within us, and living always under its care and guidance. Love to the neighbour shows itself in sympathy and in kindly regard for all men. You have now the secret of life. I need you. I long for my message to go more simply to the minds and hearts of eager, care-encumbered people. You have come through suffering. You have eaten of the husks, and now you have the real bread of life. You know now that the human spirit is divine, part and parcel of the infinite Divine life. You will grow in this realization, and growing in and living it, you will play a part in bringing others to a knowledge of the Kingdom within.'

Then turning as if he listens to something in the far distance, Jesus says: 'I shall go shortly. A ruler asks my help — earnestly he seeks to follow the Way — he is fearful and disturbed, but his heart is right. He is getting the clear vision that there is but the one Life, the Father, and that all men are brothers; that love, service, mutuality, co-operation constitute the way of life, and that until this is realized and all human relations built upon it, there is no hope in sight. When it is really learned, a new world comes in.'

The historian of the future will, I believe, point to ours as a time when a great change took place in Christendom.

Men and women, and especially young men and women, now far more free from ancestral and inherited inhibitions than any before them, begin to ask, not, do you believe this or that about the Christ? But, do you believe the things of the Christ — the things he taught? Do you sense his life and his power? Do you believe him when he states the source of his power, and when he says that the same power, under the same law, is available for all who believe his words and who follow him? A new spirit, a wonderful spirit comes into Christianity, with promise of a great religious revival throughout Christendom, more profound and vital than it has ever known.

Men and women in a growing host find God, and the peace and the power that come with the finding, and they manifest God. They realize as never before their relations one with another. They begin to understand that love is the fundamental law of the Life of the universe.

With this new vision, they begin to put love, sympathy, mutuality, and co-operation to work, so that they actually pervade their personal lives; and next their social, their community, their business and industrial lives; then the affairs of their State and nation; and finally their relations with all other nations. From their ranks comes a poet and prophet, saying:

> No matter how the die is cast, Or who may seem to win,
> We know that we must love at last - Why not begin?

This is really the culmination of what that clear-seeing writer of another nation, Victor Hugo, had in mind when he said; 'There is one thing that is stronger than armies, and that is an idea whose time has come.'

Young people in vast numbers — they who for a time seemed to their elders to be drifting on mere pleasure bent, even as the prodigal young people in vast numbers come and sit at the feet of Christ, and learn of him. They find him free, frank and open — the enemy of cant, formalism and hypocrisy in religion and life. They find him arresting and virile; in love with life, especially the life in the open, just as they are. They find a matchless love and beauty in his personality that thrills and captivates them, and draws them ever closer to him.

They find him eager to give forth life, the more abundant life, the free life of the spirit, which he, through his great faculty of discerning the laws and the things of the mind and the spirit, perceived and lived — so that he speaks to them as one having authority: the life which transformed him from Joshua Ben Joseph, the carpenter of the little village of Nazareth, to the Christ Jesus, the world Saviour.

And truly they say, as they know him better, 'He is our Saviour; for he saves us from our lower conceptions and selves. He is our Redeemer; for he redeems us from the domination, the bondage, of the senses and excesses — and the heavy bills that we eventually would have to pay. He is truly the Son of God, the Mediator; for he shows us that we too are the sons of God.

'Truly God is our Father, as well as his Father, even as he said, and we are brothers. We will be true to his teaching of the Way — to our own better selves. We will so live and work, that a new world order will come in, the Kingdom of God here on earth. For did he not say: "The Kingdom of God is at hand"? And his life, revelation, and work will bear more nearly the fruit that he so longed for — that he so magnificently lived, and so heroically died for.'

Thinking men and women the world over, sitting in an ever-larger company directly at the Master's feet, are discovering that he perceived unerringly, that he lived and taught, not a creeping-through process, but 'our Father in Heaven' — the unity, the at-one-ment, of the human spirit with the Divine. They are finding that to know God the Father, whom he so intimately knew and revealed, and to know Him as by him revealed, gives a religion of a joyous, conquering power, by virtue of the higher forces of the Divine life and power, eternally latent within, springing forward into a useful, creative, and ever-growing activity.

They believe, moreover, that he who knows God here, and gives evidence that he knows Him, by a loving, upright, manly, helpful, and humble manner of living, will be known by God, both here and hereafter, as the Master so clearly taught. They believe it because they are drawn irresistibly, as they know him better, to believe the Man Who Knew.

THE END